Brian J Robb

The Pocket Essential

RIDLEY SCOTT

www.pocketessentials.com

First published in Great Britain 2001 by Pocket Essentials, 18 Coleswood Road, Harpenden, Herts, AL5 1EQ

Distributed in the USA by Trafalgar Square Publishing, PO Box 257, Howe Hill Road, North Pomfret, Vermont 05053

Copyright © Brian J Robb 2001
Series Editor: Paul Duncan

A CIP catalogue record for this book is available from the British Library.

ISBN 1-903047-56-0

9 8 7 6 5 4 3 2 1

Book typeset by Pdunk
Printed and bound by Cox & Wyman

For Brigid and Cameron for putting up with the usual nonsense. Again.

Acknowledgements

Due recognition to Paul M Sammon, whose invaluable work on *Blade Runner* uncovered everything you'd ever need to know about that film (and then some). Thanks to the various film distributors and production offices for production notes, which proved invaluable. Finally, cheers to everyone on the Internet who maintains Frequently Asked Question sites and script sites: there are too many of you to mention, but keep up the good work. Directors like Ridley Scott deserve evangelists.

CONTENTS

1. Ridley Scott: World Builder

"I like to make worlds. I think when you look at the first four films I did – *The Duellists, Alien, Blade Runner* and *Legend* – they're all worlds. I think, really, that's what I like to do."

– Ridley Scott

There is no one else who makes movies which look and feel quite like those from director Ridley Scott. From his feature-length debut, *The Duellists* (1977), through to his triumphant return to form with *Gladiator* (2000), Scott has been a consummate creator of unique cinematic worlds.

His visualisation of other times and other places has ranged from the imaginative science fiction and fantasy environments of *Alien* (1979), *Blade Runner* (1982) and *Legend* (1985) to the recreation of the historical events of *1492: Conquest Of Paradise* (1992) and *Gladiator* (2000). For all of them he has created unique looks, but often at a commercial or personal cost: "I did a film called *1492*, which no one really saw, but that I thought was very good. That was another world. It was Columbus and the Spanish inquisition. I really enjoyed doing that."

Even Scott's relatively lesser films, like the crime dramas *Someone To Watch Over Me* (1987) and *Black Rain* (1989), the lost-at-sea adventure movie *White Squall* (1996) and the controversial woman-in-the-army drama *G. I. Jane* (1997), manage to bring unique worlds and unforgettable images to the big screen.

Despite his clear achievements in his early movies, there have been those critics who have accused Scott of producing films which may be brilliant looking, but are lacking in content and story, characters and drama. It's an accusation which has dogged Scott throughout his career, and one which some of the flashier movies of the late 1980s and early 1990s do much to support. His well-known background in the world of television advertising also fuelled this critical and popular opinion.

However, there are those who see beyond the images to the ideas behind the films. David Puttnam, producer of Ridley Scott's first movie, *The Duellists*, directly tackled these accusations: "I remember someone criticising Ridley, saying 'the images are too perfect.' It's a bit like saying to Rembrandt 'you paint too well.' In the end, he has a tremendous eye. What do you do, deny it? Pretend you don't have it?"

Many of Scott's images are indeed perfect, but some of his films are not. His output splits audiences down the middle. For every individual who loved *Alien* and *Blade Runner*, there's another who hated *White Squall* and *1492: Conquest Of Paradise*. Occasionally, they're the same people. For every feminist fan of *Thelma & Louise* (1991), there's another, equally feminist critic who despises *G. I. Jane*. The engagement which these audiences have with the films of Ridley Scott clearly shows that the style-versus-substance argument is a red herring.

The more important question about Ridley Scott and his films is how under the guise of producing mainstream, often blockbuster, movies he has managed to create such distinctive and individual works laden with effective political and social criticism.

He is a British director who has played the movie game the way they do in Hollywood; a creator of unique films who is also something of an old-style film mogul with his advertising production house Ridley Scott Associates, his film production company Scott Free and his ownership interests in Britain's Shepperton Studios and the Mill Film Ltd effects house. He's a film-maker who is also a canny businessman. In fact, it's possible his interest in the business side of film-making has detracted from the films he has made over the years.

Ridley Scott embodies the idea of director as architect, a builder of worlds, both of individual films and of a mini film-making empire. Despite his training as a production designer and his emphasis on the visual (after all, what are movies if not a primarily visual medium?) Scott does pay great attention to the scripts for each of his films. "Every film is a different experience in terms of how you come to the most important thing, which is the script," noted Scott. "The script is the blueprint of the building. If you don't have it on paper at some point in time, the 'building' is not going to stand."

Producer David Puttnam noted the director's "erratic greatness" and feared that he contributed to his own problems. "Ridley is always in a hurry to shoot," claimed Puttnam. "Although he knows that a script may have flaws, he will rely on his immense technical virtuosity to cover them over."

In his quest for new stories to tell, Scott has often drawn on literary sources for his most visual films: from Joseph Conrad for *The Duellists*; Philip K Dick for *Blade Runner* and Thomas Harris for *Hannibal* (2001) to the fact-based films *White Squall* and *G. I. Jane* and the historical tales *1492: Conquest Of Paradise* and *Gladiator*. However, it is the 'look' of the movie that takes precedence over everything else, arguably even including the performances. "There are certain moments," the director once claimed, "where the background can be as important as the actor." Despite that, Scott has a knack for spotting and using actors who will later become stars:

8

Harvey Keitel, Sigourney Weaver, Harrison Ford, Darryl Hannah, Tom Cruise, Andy Garcia, Brad Pitt, Ryan Phillippe and James Caviezel have all gone on to bigger things after featuring in a Ridley Scott film.

Ridley Scott is always at his best when he finds a subject matter which suits his style. Of all his films to date, the science fiction/fantasy trilogy of *Alien, Blade Runner* and *Legend* have seen the perfect match between subject and style and hence gain more attention than much of his other work. The recent *Gladiator* showed that he could finally achieve what he'd failed to do before with *1492: Conquest Of Paradise*: a fusion between historical fiction and his extravagant visuals. The mix of his visual style with more contemporary and down-to-earth settings and stories has been somewhat uneasy, explaining the poor critical and commercial showings for *Someone To Watch Over Me, Black Rain* (almost a contemporary remake of *Blade Runner*) and *White Squall*. The one major oddity in his career was *Thelma & Louise*, the only film where he reined in his visual excesses and allowed the performances, politics and story to dominate. Outside of his science-fiction epics and *Gladiator, Thelma & Louise* was Scott's most successful film. It might be a lesson for the future, one he has brought to bear on his film of Thomas Harris' *Hannibal*, the follow-up to the Oscar-winning *The Silence Of The Lambs*.

Gladiator finally saw Ridley Scott return to form after a series of disappointing (both critically and commercially) films. Scott is torn between his need to produce hit commercial films and his desire to create movies which stand the test of time. *Blade Runner* is rightly acclaimed as a classic, but many people forget it was a huge commercial flop in 1982. There is time yet for neglected films like *Black Rain* and *1492: Conquest Of Paradise* to be rediscovered by appreciative audiences. In the meantime, Scott will continue his balancing act of creating unique worlds and producing successful films. It's a task he's uniquely cut out for.

2. Beginnings

Childhood

Ridley Scott was born on 30 November 1937 as the middle brother of three. His mother and father, Elizabeth and Francis Percy Scott, already had one son named Frank (who was to die of a cancer-related illness in 1980) and would later have a third, Tony (who would follow in his brother's footsteps as a movie director).

Scott's father Francis Percy (more commonly referred to as Frank by the family) had been a partner in a successful shipping business which had been brought to a halt with the outbreak of World War Two, then he joined the army as an NCO. Scott recalled that "during the last two years of World War Two, [my father] was attached to the War Office, and associated with Churchill. He also spent time working on an operation to help get our troops into Normandy."

Later in life, Scott would claim his mother as one of his strongest influences. "She's 95 and still going strong," he said in the year 2000 when the director himself was 62. "During World War Two, when my father was away fighting, she had to do the work of both parents. That's where I get this admiration for powerful women [in my films]."

Frank stayed on in the army and the military lifestyle led to an unsettled life as the family moved from posting to posting in the years after the war. Although born in South Shields in the north-east of England, Scott lived as far afield as London, Cumbria and even Wales in the years from 1947 until about 1952, when Scott's father finally retired from the military and returned to Stockton-on-Tees and the shipping business.

Although military-inspired discipline was central to the family, so too was a tolerance for individual artistic expression. Scott's father was something of a frustrated artist, often to be found doodling with his pen and ink. Like many children, Scott was interested in comics, but his interest extended to studying the composition of the individual comic panels, examining the positioning of the characters and working out how the lighting effects had been achieved. According to the original press notes issued for the film *Blade Runner*, Ridley Scott "showed little scholastic aptitude for any subject but art." It was typical of his parents, Frank and Elizabeth, that they didn't try and force Scott to follow a particular vocation or even to join his father in the shipping business. According to Scott, becoming a teacher or a lawyer was the expected career route for children of his class and education. Instead, he wanted to become a stage designer.

The stage was calling Scott, not cinema. "It was all rather ordinary," claimed Scott of his childhood cinema trips. "It wasn't as if films were the great passion of my life. I'd go with my family or mates and sit in the dark and watch whatever was playing that week." Scott didn't recall any individual films which made an impact on him. Instead, he remembered the sense of community among the cinema audience, the fact that during musicals people would sing along or get carried away during a thriller and call out warnings to the characters on screen. It was this pseudo-audience participation (something more often experienced in the live theatre) which captured Scott's imagination.

Although his parents supported his decision to attend art college, Scott was also encouraged by one schoolteacher who told him to follow his skill and develop his own innate talents. So, in 1954 Scott found himself attending West Hartlepool College of Art, about 30 miles south of his birthplace. Four years at art college taught Ridley Scott to become adept with pencil and paper in sketching and developing his skills as a painter, but he learned so much more about life and other arts. He discovered music, literature and the popular culture shown on television. Away from the family home for the first time and able to immerse himself in topics which he thoroughly enjoyed, Scott found himself developing his own opinions on issues of the day and his own unique view of the world.

Further Education

Aged 20, Ridley Scott graduated from West Hartlepool College of Art. It was 1958 and National Service – compulsory military service for the country's youth in Britain's post-war years – was calling. Given the military background in his family and his own disinclination to follow the academic life, Scott felt four years of what he called "brainbashing" was more than enough and it was time for him to do his bit for his country as his father had. Opposition to this course of action came from a most unexpected source: Frank Scott.

Scott's father felt his son was in danger of wasting his talents. By this time it was clear to everyone that Ridley Scott was an accomplished painter and draughtsman. He'd actually graduated with Honours, meaning it would have been relatively easy for him to have pursued a career in academia or teaching. Scott was ready to enlist in the Marines for the mandatory two-year service when his father persuaded him to defer his National Service in order to pursue his studies.

Having developed a stubborn and opinionated streak while at college, Scott was prepared to argue his corner. It was the offer of a scholarship from the prestigious London-based Royal College of Art (RCA) which gave Scott pause for thought. He was aware of the reputation of the RCA as a dynamic and progressive art school, a reputation it still enjoys today. The generous scholarship would take care of any money worries and the chance to further develop his growing skills was too good to turn down. He was encouraged to apply for a place at the RCA and was delighted when he won through and started studying there during the autumn of 1958.

Although recruited to the RCA as a graphic designer, the set-up at the college was such that students could try a bit of everything, without a requirement to stick to their specialisation. Ridley Scott found himself exploring the possibilities of sculpture, alongside those of photography, painting and sketching, even applied industrial design. The atmosphere at the RCA provided the young Ridley Scott with the perfect melting pot for artistic ideas, and the 20-year-old was like a sponge, ready to absorb as many influences as possible. The RCA was also where Ridley Scott was to discover the possibilities of cinema. "I really only became a hard-core movie buff, in a serious fashion, when I came to the RCA and London," Scott told one interviewer. "I used to spend every weekend in the National Film Theatre or places like the Academy Cinema on Oxford Street, where I was suddenly seeing all types of cinema." The late 1950s and early 1960s were a tremendously exciting time for cinema. The French New Wave had been incredibly influential, an influence which would be seen in American/ Hollywood cinema throughout the 1960s and 1970s. Italian post-war neo-realism was being converted into the kitchen sink dramas of UK cinema. In London, the theatre, from which the Angry Young Man movement had emerged, was beginning to influence cinema through a new strand of bleak social realism. Scott began to identify the work of individual directors, becoming a fan of Swedish director Ingmar Bergman. Hollywood cinema was also a big attraction, with Scott particularly enjoying westerns.

Scott could not see how he – a mere art student – could begin to make inroads into the world of movie-making. Britain did not have a dedicated film school at that time and the only way Scott could see to break into the movies was to be born in California or have a relation already in the industry. Television, however, was a different matter.

In his last year at the RCA, Scott enrolled in two additional postgraduate courses which he felt might allow him to make a start in the world of British television. Television in the UK had just opened up to competition with the state-funded BBC facing the commercial Independent Television network from 1955. There were opportunities in this new world for those with the right background. With that in mind Scott signed up for courses in scenic design, then still under the guise of 'theatre design', in the hope of finding a way into television.

First Film

A chance discovery further fuelled Scott's growing interest in the practicalities of film and television production. While searching through a cupboard in the RCA's Theatre Design department he came across a bizarre object which turned out to be a Bolex 16mm cine-camera, complete with an instruction manual and even a light meter. The unused camera meant only one thing to Scott: he could make his own film. Soon he had permission from the college to borrow the camera and set about studying the manual to see how to work the thing. With a budget of about £65 to cover all his costs, including buying film, paying for processing and recording the sound, this debut film was not going to be the kind of epic which Scott would later be known for.

Scott knew enough about film-making to be aware that he needed a script, or in this case a scenario. He had a basic idea about a young boy who skips off school for a day, exploring a seaside town by bike. The star of the film was his brother, Tony Scott, then 16 years old. Starting with a domestic scene, the 27-minute film follows the "Tony" character as he leaves the house, decides not to go to school and instead partakes of the various pleasures of 1950s seaside towns: buying candy; smoking a cigarette; visiting the funfair and the beach, both strangely deserted. The discovery of a dead dog and an abandoned hut add texture to the film, and the return of the tramp who lives there causes Tony to make an escape on his bicycle.

The simply titled 16mm film, *Boy And Bicycle*, was a real Scott family affair. As well as brother Tony, the film featured his father Frank as the frightening tramp and his mother Elizabeth as Tony's mother. Scott storyboarded every single scene of the film, a habit he was to maintain for most of his film-making career. Scott was also developing other techniques and cinematic tricks which he would put to good use later in his career. "I was heavily into Kurosawa at the time," he admitted. "I knew he used certain filters for his monochrome films. So I was stuffing on red filters every chance I got. I used a lot of hand-held camera, and even drafted my father to act as a camera-car driver."

At heart, *Boy And Bicycle* is an arty, documentary social realist indulgence with a few small signs of what audiences could later expect from a Ridley Scott film. The film had been shot over six weeks in 1961, with voice-over and synchronised dialogue added later. The first audiences for

Boy And Bicycle were Scott's teachers and fellow students in the Theatre Design department of the RCA. The film was one of five produced by the students, none of which seem to have been particularly remarkable (Scott's effort included).

That would have been that for *Boy And Bicycle*, except for a curious footnote. Long after Scott had graduated from the RCA and moved onto other things, he got a call from one of the department's new tutors. They had a £250 grant from the British Film Institute and wanted Scott to return and finish the post-production sound on his film properly. Scott agreed, adding sound effects and clearing up some of the audio on the voice-over. There was one problem, though. Not expecting the film ever to be seen commercially, Scott had used a brief piece of music from film score composer John Barry. He couldn't afford to pay for the rights to use the music, even with the BFI's £250, so he asked Barry for a favour. As a composer on the rise, Barry was busy. Yet he was taken by this youngster and agreed to record a new version of the music Scott wanted. "That's how John Barry came to record some music for my first film," recalled Scott. The film was then screened as part of a series of works presented by the BFI's Experimental Film Fund. *Boy And Bicycle* has been retained by the BFI as a significant short film to this day.

The Budding Director

"By the time I was 19," claimed Scott, "I'd seriously begun thinking of myself as a film director." It was an ambition he wasn't to achieve for a while, as he had other artistic distractions. "I was still drawn to advertising and set design. I didn't quite know how I'd become a director, but I figured I'd be one step closer if I could get a job designing sets for the BBC."

Scott graduated from the Royal College of Art in 1961 and applied to the BBC, while still considering other career options in graphic design and advertising. He was accepted by the BBC but, at the same time, he was offered a travelling scholarship in design, which would take him to New York and a job with Bob Drew Associates, one of the city's top advertising agencies. Ridley Scott had a choice to make.

Unusually enough, the problem was solved for him when the BBC offered to hold the position in their scenic design department open for 12 months. That would give Scott enough time to make the most of the scholarship funds and then return to the job in London at the end of it. This was an ideal solution and one the would-be director jumped at.

Scott's time at Bob Drew Associates was brief, but it was long enough to indicate to him that perhaps the worlds of advertising and fashion were not for him after all. Documentary film-making caught his attention and he'd soon talked himself into a job with D A Pennebaker and Richard Leacock, then making acclaimed short documentary films for Time/Life Inc. He spent eight months or so learning all he could about film editing. While there, the BBC began to apply pressure for Scott to return to London and take up his job in scenic design. He was faced with another choice: opt for the secure BBC job or continue to explore the insecure world of New York film-making?

There was no real indecision for the young Englishman abroad. After a few more weeks travelling across the United States, Scott returned to the UK and walked into his new career at the BBC.

At The BBC

By 1962 Ridley Scott was a fully-fledged art director at the BBC having bypassed the usual period as an assistant due to his education and experience. He quickly learned how the BBC worked, how to deal with the bureaucracy and how to maximise his creativity on a strictly controlled budget. Over the next few years he would spend his time designing and creating a whole range of sets for a variety of BBC television programmes, from weekly variety shows to serious heavyweight dramas and sitcoms. Scott learned how to work as part of a larger organisation, how to make the system work for him, not against him. These were valuable lessons, but ones which he nevertheless would not always be able to apply to his dealings with the Hollywood studios when it came to making his own feature films.

"All the time I was at the BBC I was like a human sponge," said Scott. "I was soaking it all up. I was working alongside the director, the producer, the lighting people... the BBC fundamentally taught me to know what I wanted, how to communicate and organise." He was, however, frustrated by being just a designer and really wanted to direct: "I was doing patterns on a screen," he said of his work on the BBC current affair programme *Tonight*. "Seven years at art school and I was doing patterns on a screen..."

By 1963, Scott was back to indulging his interest in the growing field of advertising. He was moonlighting, effectively, topping up his BBC income with the bigger earnings available in the British television commercials business. Designing and dressing sets for commercials, above and beyond his BBC work, soon led to an offer to direct. The ad that saw Ridley Scott step behind the camera for the first time professionally was a typical 1960s effort promoting baby food.

Scott wasn't just moonlighting for the experience or the chance to turn director: he was now married and had a large mortgage to pay off. While enrolled at the RCA, Scott had met and married a fellow arts student. By the time he was at the BBC in 1963, he had a new house and ever increasing bills. He was also moving further towards fulfilling his directorial ambitions within the BBC. Aware of his desire to move behind the camera and call the shots, his bosses sent Scott on the famous BBC residential directors course. Locked away in a country location at the BBC Training Centre, Wood Norton in Hereford and Worcester, Scott learned to direct the BBC way. At the end of the course, he was set a task: he had to bring in a production of his choice under BBC conditions and to a BBC budget. Scott characterised his experiences during this time as: "Marvellous training, really."

Scott chose to film a half hour version of *Paths Of Glory*, a novel by Humphrey Cobb previously filmed in 1957 by Stanley Kubrick. Scott became something of a one-man TV production machine, writing the script, designing the sets, selecting props as well as directing the work, finally shooting the whole thing with a borrowed 35mm camera. Scott roped in actor Keith Barron, a friend, to star in the production free of charge, thus contributing towards his attempts to produce something spectacular on the infamously frugal BBC budgets.

As was standard in BBC TV production at the time, Scott's *Paths Of Glory* was rehearsed once in the afternoon, then shot in a series of long takes that same evening. Scott described the day as "a bit terrifying." One of his problems was communicating exactly what he wanted to the production staff around him, despite his experience as a designer having shown him that this kind of communication was key to the process. This difficulty in having others realise his visual ideas was to return when Scott was making bigger budget feature films.

Despite his problems with the production of *Paths Of Glory*, it served its purpose and brought Scott to the attention of Tony Giles, a BBC producer with his eye out for new directing talent. He contacted Scott about directing an episode of the BBC police drama *Softly, Softly*, a spin-off from the popular police series *Z-Cars*. As was still widely practised at the time, *Softly, Softly* was a live show. Given three weeks to prepare the show, Scott threw himself into the job with abandon. While Scott was worrying about prepping a live TV broadcast, a nerve-wracking event in itself, the wider world was dealing with the unfolding Cuban missile crisis. Despite his worries, the broadcast was a success and led to Scott being invited back to direct several episodes in a row. "By now I was getting the hang of directing for television," he noted. "I eased into broadcast directing fairly easily." Success with *Softly, Softly* led to further opportunities, including an episode of *The Informer* starring Ian Hendry, *Z-Cars* and *Adam Adamant Lives!* However, Scott was beginning to learn the limitations of directing for black-and-white 405-line television. The attractions of the expensive, high production value 60-second commercials was proving to be a strong lure once again. Here's one example of Scott's 1960s TV output:

Adam Adamant Lives! (1966)

'The League Of Uncharitable Ladies'

Director: Ridley Scott, Writer: John Pennington

Cast: Adam Adamant (Gerald Harper), Georgina Jones (Juliet Harmer), William E Simms (Jack May), Prudence (Geraldine Moffat), Abstinence (Eve Gross), Jarrott (Gerald Sim), Charity (Amelia Baynton), Hope (Sheila Grant), Faith (Lucy Griffiths), Randolph (John Carson)

Crew: Producer: Verity Lambert; Created by Don Cotton, Richard Harris; Script Editor: Tony Williamson; Designer: Mary Rea; Music: David Lee; Fight Arranger: Ian McKay; Editor: Valerie Best

Plot: A murder in St James' Park leads investigator Adam Adamant to a strange women's club in Pall Mall, and a committee of three old ladies called Faith, Hope and Charity, who are not what their names imply.

The Episode: Modelled after *The Avengers*, *Adam Adamant Lives!* was a short-lived BBC series which chronicled the adventures of gentleman adventurer Adam Adamant, frozen in the Victorian era and defrosted in the swinging 60s. As well as much culture clash humour, especially with his liberated sidekick Georgina Jones, the series featured much swashbuckling adventure and investigation of very eccentric cases.

Eccentric could describe 'The League of Uncharitable Ladies,' Scott's first directorial outing for the series. This tale is about an exclusive ladies club which signs up the wives of the great and the good, then hypnotises them into assassinating their husbands.

From the opening sequence (the murder in Pall Mall) it is clear that this episode is helmed by a director to watch. The whole sequence is silent, except for bird sounds. Scott's camera follows the victim through Pall Mall, tracking him through the park, and shooting into the sun or bright light (a technique Scott developed through his advertising work). The climax is shot from the victim's point of view, with the camera spinning in circles. From fluid movement, to shaky, hand-held techniques, the camera never stops moving. The influence of *Boy And Bicycle* is clear here. Even boring office-bound scenes of exposition are spiced up by Scott's restless camera. Shots of cars moving from location to location look down on the bonnets or feature shots of passing architectural curiosities, including along Pall Mall and through Piccadilly Circus.

Scott, however, can't keep this inventiveness up forever, and as the episode moves on to more interior scenes, his directorial flourishes are less evident, with the need to get the story told and concluded taking precedence. He does, however, finish the piece off with a freeze-frame ending.

For *Adam Adamant Lives!* Scott also directed two further episodes: 'Death Begins at Seventy', set in an old folks home, and 'The Resurrectionists', which saw Adamant investigating a scientist who is an agent of his arch enemy, The Face. "I was one of two or three directors who did *Adam Adamant Lives!* – the *Batman* of Kensington with Gerald Harper. That was great fun."

Ridley Scott Associates

In 1964 Ridley Scott was only 27 years old, but he'd left his position at the BBC, ready to make his way in the world of advertising. Success here came quickly and easily as Scott's rapidly developing visual style, which he was able to indulge in the well-funded advertising world, was much in demand. So much so that Scott became tired of being a director for hire. The work was certainly lucrative and he was allowed the scope to develop some of his directorial ideas, but he had no stake in the success or failure of the business side of his advertising work. With one eye on the future, Scott knew that the only way he could have control over the work he did was to secure it through his own company. Thus, Ridley Scott Associates (RSA) was born.

The company was set up in 1965 and is still going strong today. It wasn't plain sailing at the beginning, though, as it took a while for RSA to build up a strong client base. Scott was so busy that he had to bring in hired help, starting with his brother. Tony Scott had also recently graduated from the RCA with two student films under his belt. Although initially resistant to throwing his lot in with his older brother, the younger Scott eventually capitulated and joined what was rapidly becoming a family firm. Other British feature film directors to have done stints with Scott at RSA included Hugh Hudson and Peter Webb.

Scott often wore his influences on his sleeve, indulging his art education through the 3000-plus commercials he directed for RSA up until the mid-1970s. Among the adverts he was responsible for were several award winners, including films for Levi's Jeans, Strongbow Cider and the famous Hovis Bread ad.

The Duellists (1977)

Director: Ridley Scott, Writers: Joseph Conrad (story *The Duel*), Gerald Vaughan-Hughes

Cast: Keith Carradine (Armand d'Hubert), Harvey Keitel (Gabriel Féraud), Albert Finney (Fouche), Edward Fox (Colonel), Cristina Raines (Adèle), Robert Stephens (General Treillard), Tom Conti (Dr. Jacquin), John McEnery (Chevalier), Diana Quick (Laura), Alun Armstrong (Lacourbe), Maurice Colbourne (Second), Gay Hamilton (Maid), Meg Wynn Owen (Leonie), Jenny Runacre (Mme. de Lionne), Alan Webb (Chevalier), W Morgan Sheppard, Liz Smith, Pete Postlethwaite, Jason Scott, Luke Scott, Stacy Keach (Narrator voice)

Crew: Producer: David Puttnam; Music: Howard Blake; Cinematography: Frank Tidy; Editing: Michael Bradsell, Pamela Power; Production Design: Peter J Hampton; Art Direction: Bryan Graves; Continuity: Kay Fenton; Fight Arranger: William Hobbs; Camera Operator: Ridley Scott

Plot: Two officers in Napoleon's 7th Hussars, one of noble birth with connections (d'Hubert), the other common born (Féraud), rise up through the ranks as the wars progress until the defeat of Napoleon and the restoration of the Bourbon monarchy put an end to their careers. Although their paths do not cross very often, whenever they meet they fight a duel (with swords or pistols), the continuation of some earlier slight which neither seems able to remember exactly.

Inspiration: By this time Scott had a young family, with his wife and two sons: Jason and Luke. His business was a success and making adverts was fulfilling some of his creative ambitions. However, the possibilities of feature-film-making continued to be attractive. One of the driving forces for Scott was a kind of rivalry that was developing between himself and several other ad directors who were moving over to movie-making. Among them were Alan Parker, who'd already embarked on some movie projects, and RSA director Hugh Hudson.

Scott began developing a script in 1971 for a heist movie to be called *Running In Place*. Although the project did attract funding and the interest of British actor Michael York, it collapsed quite quickly when the promised cash evaporated. In 1972, Scott hired writer John Edwards to develop *Castle X*, which Scott described as "a Medieval horror film." It drew the attention of pop stars the Bee Gees, but again, promised financing failed to materialise.

Further scripts were developed by Scott with various writing partners throughout the 1970s, including one based on the Guy Fawkes Gunpowder Plot of 1605 and another about a 19th century palaeontologist who photographed dinosaur fossils around America.

By the mid-1970s, Scott was turning back to television for directorial opportunities away from commercials. He formed a relationship with French company Technicinol, who were producing a series of literary adaptations. Initially Scott was interested in making a film of a Henry James' short story, but he soon switched his attention to *The Duel*, a short story by Joseph Conrad, author of *Heart Of Darkness* (the inspiration for Francis Ford Coppola's *Apocalypse Now* which was then shooting in the Philippines). Scott found himself with a £150,000 budget and an offer to direct a one-hour version of *The Duel* for French television. It wasn't quite the feature film he'd wanted, but it was a start. The project, though, was about to metamorphose.

Writer Gerald Vaughan-Hughes, whom Scott had been working with and who had an interest in history, scripted the film and called it *The Duellists*. The script so impressed Scott and the money men behind the project that they began discussing the possibility of expanding it into a full length feature film intended for cinema distribution rather than television broadcast. French firm Technicinol were not able to fund the estimated £700,000 budget required for a film version of *The Duel*, but British music and movies company EMI and American Hallmark Hall of Fame executives were interested in the project. Again, the film proved too costly a prospect for either company.

Scott finally found a home for *The Duellists* at Enigma, a film production company being run by producer David Puttnam. Impressed by the script, Puttnam was convinced he could put together the funding package. "I started working with Ridley to develop a couple of screenplays," recalled Puttnam. "We had what became *The Duellists*, and *The Gunpowder Plot*. [Alan] Parker's *Bugsy Malone* was presented at Cannes and was an absolutely phenomenal success. As I left the cinema the guy from Paramount, David Picker, said 'This is an extraordinary talent. Do you know anyone else like him?' And I said, 'A chap called Ridley Scott.' So he said, 'I'd like to meet him.'" That was enough of an invitation for Puttnam to pull in Scott. "I went straight from the cinema, phoned Ridley at home, told him to jump on a plane first thing tomorrow morning. Lunchtime the following day we were on the beach – this is a Cannes story par excellence – making a deal. When we got to the crux of what film we were going to do (we had the two scripts) I said one will cost $2 million and one we can make for $1.2 million and Picker said, 'I'll take the cheaper one.' We both nodded. Six months later we were making *The Duellists*."

Production: With a final budget just shy of $1 million and a less than wholehearted commitment from the studio to this 'little' project, Scott determined to go ahead immediately and shoot the film through the winter months, a proposal which alarmed the studio. "I was afraid this thing would never happen if we waited until spring," admitted Scott of his motivation for plunging almost foolhardily into making *The Duellists*.

The film was officially given the green light, and Scott was able to turn his attention to casting, while Puttnam looked after the more practical elements of the production like hiring equipment, studio space and securing location permissions. Scott was able to recruit his first choice actors to playing the feuding main characters in the film: Keith Carradine and Harvey Keitel. Both were enjoying a period of fame and fortune, with recent films like *Thieves Like Us, Nashville, Mean Streets* and *Taxi Driver*.

Drawing on his BBC and commercials experience, Scott recruited a who's who of British actors of the mid-1970s for supporting roles in the film, including Edward Fox, Tom Conti, Pete Postlethwaite, Robert Stephens, Jenny Runacre and Diana Quick. A coup was signing up Albert Finney for a small part in return for a case of champagne.

The Duellists was shot between September and Christmas 1976 at locations across northern Scotland (standing in for the Russian Steppes), and the medieval town of Sarlat in the Dordogne area of France. "I learned to stop worrying before I'd done my first feature," claimed Scott. "I'd worked so much in commercial advertising, filming under all kinds of conditions, where the buck stops with you once you take the job on. I loved the long form and by that time I'd exorcised the fear. I found the whole process quite easy."

Scott brought all his design and art background to bear on the look of *The Duellists*, but the biggest influence was a 1975 Stanley Kubrick film called *Barry Lyndon*. There were other direct influences. "The best references on any period in history are its painters. So, before we shot, I started to look at the Napoleonic painters and other artists, for lighting effects." Scott also storyboarded every scene of the film, just as he had for his commercials and television productions.

Reception: By the middle of 1977, Ridley Scott was finishing off post-production on his first feature film. All of a sudden, Paramount Pictures showed renewed interest in this small, low-budget film which the studio had funded. Paramount executives Barry Diller and Michael Eisner were impressed by what they saw when Scott screened an in-progress print of the film in Los Angeles. With the studio now firmly behind the little film they'd almost forgotten about, *The Duellists* was screened at the 1977 Cannes Film Festival, walking away with the Special Jury Prize in the process. Good critical reviews followed. Film critic Geoff Andrew called the film 'visually sumptuous', while the *Variety* review characterised Scott's debut movie as having 'definite flair', while Scott himself 'does have an eye for fine composition, period recreation and arresting tableaux', concluding that the film was an 'arty swashbuckler'.

Despite the success of *The Duellists* as a film in its own right and the positive nature of the reviews, the distribution of the film in America through 1978 did little to please the director. "I wasn't happy at all with its release," he complained. "Paramount put out seven prints of *The Duellists* and it only played one cinema in all of Los Angeles. *The Duellists* was not an art film: while shooting, I thought of it as a western. Yet, it was booked on the art-house circuit, so it never reached the large-scale audience it was intended for."

As he turned 40, Ridley Scott had finally achieved what had been an ambition since his arrival at art school: he'd become a bona fide film director.

Facts And Figures:

• The film conveys the idea of private war within a much larger public war and examines the nature of male aggression: why do men fight duels, go to war, fight in pubs on Friday nights? The issue of honour and 'getting satisfaction' when honour is slighted is also examined.

• The swords were hooked up to batteries to produce the sparks, and Harvey Keitel said he was heavily shocked more than once.

• The six duels featured in *The Duellists* follow closely the major battles and occupations of Europe by Napoleon's forces: Strasbourg 1800, Augsburg 1801, Lübeck 1806, Spain 1808, Russia 1812, Tours 1814.

3. The Science Fiction Trilogy

Alien (1979)

"You still don't know what you're dealing with do you? The perfect organism. Its structural perfection is matched only by its hostility. I admire its purity, a survivor; unclouded by conscience, remorse or delusions of morality."

- Ash, *Alien.*

Director: Ridley Scott, Writers: Dan O'Bannon, David Giler (Uncredited) & Walter Hill (Uncredited), Story: Dan O'Bannon & Ronald Shusett

Cast: Tom Skerritt (Captain Dallas), Sigourney Weaver (Warrant Officer Ellen Ripley), Veronica Cartwright (Navigation Officer Lambert), Harry Dean Stanton (Engineer Brett), John Hurt (Executive Officer Kane), Ian Holm (Science Officer Ash), Yaphet Kotto (Engineer Parker), Bolaji Badejo (The Alien), Helen Horton (voice of "Mother"), Eddie Powell (Stunt Alien), Percy Edwards (Alien Vocals, Uncredited)

Crew: Producers: Gordon Carroll, David Giler, Walter Hill, Ivor Powell (Associate), Ronald Shusett (Executive); Music: Jerry Goldsmith, Howard Hanson (from '2. Symphony'), Wolfgang Amadeus Mozart (from 'Eine kleine Nachtmusik'); Cinematography: Derek Vanlint; Editing: Terry Rawlings, Peter Weatherley; Production Design: Roger Christian (Uncredited), Anton Furst (Uncredited), Michael Seymour; Art Direction: Roger Christian, Leslie Dilley; Costume Design: John Mollo; Special Effects Supervisor: Nick Allder; Concept Artists: Ron Cobb, Chris Foss, H R Giger, Jean Giraud

Plot: On the way home from a mission for the Company, the Nostromo's crew is woken up from hibernation by the ship's computer – called Mother – to answer a distress signal from a nearby planet. Captain Dallas sends in an investigation team who discover a bizarre pod field. A facehugging creature bursts out of a pod and attaches itself to Kane. Over the objections of Ripley, science officer Ash lets Kane back on the ship. The acid-blooded creature detaches itself from an apparently recovered Kane, but an alien erupts from Kane's stomach and escapes. The alien grows rapidly and starts stalking the humans, pitting Dallas and his crew (and the cat, Jones) against a malevolent killing machine that also has a protector in the nefarious Company.

Inspiration: Having achieved his aim of directing a feature film, one that was critically acclaimed, if not commercially successful, Ridley Scott faced a new challenge: the often difficult second feature film.

For Scott, the subject matter was paramount. He'd already given some thought to what he'd like to tackle next while on location in France shooting *The Duellists*. In the Dordogne, the beautiful locations saw Scott's thoughts turn classical. "I thought, 'My God, this is a romantic place. In fact, it's the perfect place to be thinking about a subject like *Tristan And Isolde*.' I talked to David Puttnam about making *Tristan* my next film, and Gerry Vaughan-Hughes [who'd written the screenplay for *The Duellists*] prepared a *Tristan* screenplay for us."

This Medieval romance poem, drawn from a Celtic legend, told of Tristan's wooing of Isolde, before falling foul of a love potion meant for others. Seeing the potential in the film, Paramount put the screenplay into development in 1977, with Scott operating from a Los Angeles-based production office.

While the project was to eventually fall apart, the pursuit of *Tristan And Isolde* did serve one useful purpose: it saw *The Duellists* Associate Producer Ivor Powell introduce Ridley Scott to science fiction. Powell was brought onto *Tristan And Isolde* to coordinate the production from London. He was a science fiction buff with an interest in comic books, being a fan in particular of the French publication *Métal Hurlant*, known in English as *Heavy Metal*.

More than aware of Scott's interest in art and design, Powell couldn't believe that Scott had not heard of *Heavy Metal*. For his part, Scott couldn't believe what he was seeing when he took the time to check out the vibrant, lively and downright sexy art of the comic book. "Bloody hell," he was quoted as saying. "Why don't they make films like this?"

Heavy Metal was the first part of a science fiction double whammy which was to bowl Ridley Scott over. "I was in Hollywood in the summer of 1977," recalled Scott. "David Puttnam said to me, 'Why don't we go see this new film? I understand it's pretty good.' So we trooped down to Mann's Chinese Theatre and saw this thing called *Star Wars*. It impressed me so much! It was innovative, sensitive, courageous – I saw it on three consecutive days and it didn't diminish at all. I consider it to be a milestone film – one of the 10 best I've ever seen. I was most struck by how Lucas took what is essentially a fairy tale and made it seem totally real. The combination of *2001* – a threshold film that presented science fiction as I thought it should be – and *Star Wars*, convinced me that there was a great future in science-fiction films."

This instinctive move away from art-house fare was to lay the path of a populist film-making career for Ridley Scott. Seeing *Star Wars* caused Scott to consider his potential audience: "I thought, 'Here is this guy [George Lucas] doing this and I'm thinking of doing *Tristan And Isolde*? I must be out of my mind. I'm never going to get an audience like this – this [*Star Wars*] is what cinema is about. Cinema is about taking people on an adventure for two and a half hours where they are entirely taken into that world." Scott would most successfully achieve this aim in *Blade Runner* and *Gladiator*.

In the first film of the George Lucas space-opera saga, Ridley Scott saw a reflection of the *Heavy Metal* sensibility which he was endeavouring to bring to *Tristan And Isolde*. Seeing the success of *Star Wars* and realising that the *Heavy Metal* approach would simply not work in his historical romantic project, Ridley Scott began looking around for something else, something harder-edged and drawn from science fiction.

Development: It was Sandy Leiberson, head of 20th Century Fox in the UK, who brought the script for *Alien* to the attention of Ridley Scott. Leiberson had been impressed by *The Duellists* which he'd seen at a screening at the Cannes Film Festival. Looking out for projects with which he could secure the services of Scott, Leiberson settled on a script which had endured something of a tortured history.

Originally entitled *Star Beast*, the creature-picks-off-spaceship-crew plot was originally dreamt up by writer Dan O'Bannon as a low-budget project he could direct and his partner Ron Shusett could produce. Several drafts later and a title change to *Alien* saw the project taken up by Brandywine, a production company run by writers/directors Walter Hill and David Giler with producer Gordon Carroll. Sensing the commercial possibilities of this '*Jaws* in space' movie, Giler and Hill rewrote O'Bannon's screenplay, using the same storyline but totally revamping the dialogue and action. One of the major changes was to make Ripley, the hero of the piece, a female character. It was this script that found its way to Ridley Scott via Sandy Leiberson.

Although Scott was soon to be pigeon-holed as a 'science fiction director', he was largely disparaging of the genre: "Fantasies don't work unless they quickly take on a reality of their own, and the sci-fi films I'd seen always contained silly, utopian ideas or tended to take the more extraordinary dilemmas of the day and assume they'd develop in non-logical, unbelievable ways," said Scott. "The people who made sci-fi films didn't understand what they were doing."

Despite his views, Scott took the approach from Leiberson seriously. "I'd only seen a handful of SF pictures: *The Day The Earth Stood Still, 2001, Star Wars*. As a rule, I didn't really like science-fiction pictures – they seemed pretty silly to me..."

There were, however, several elements to the screenplay which caught Scott's imagination. He found himself responding to the visual possibilities the action offered, conjuring up images in his mind as he read the script. He found the characters to be intriguing and likeable, and was especially struck by the class division between the officers on the ship and the engineering crew, especially Brett and Parker. The political machinations of the corporation behind the mission and the fact that the hero was female also proved attractive. By the time he'd finished reading the script, Scott was hooked and he knew that *Alien* had to be his next film project. "When I read the *Alien* script," recalled Scott, "not only was I fascinated by the marvellous, strong, simple narrative, but also I realised that because of my brief education reading *Heavy Metal*, I knew how to do the film. I accepted *Alien* almost immediately."

David Puttnam thought this was the right decision for Scott, rather than pursuing an art-house agenda. He saw Scott as one of a group of film directors who emerged in the late 1960s and early 1970s. "They had a visual sense which was a significant step on from the generation before them. Don't forget that there was not much of a gap between them and the Tony Richardson-Karel Reisz generation. I think the films just looked more handsome, because they didn't come from a documentary tradition. One of the reasons I didn't carry on working with Ridley was because I had a hankering to make films that were more gritty: *Midnight Express, The Killing Fields*. He wanted to make *Alien* - I had no interest in science fiction. I think on balance he was right."

Production: By February 1978, Ridley Scott was confirmed as the director of *Alien* after Walter Hill, who'd originally been attached to direct the project when it was given the go-ahead by Fox's Alan Ladd Jr. late in 1977, moved onto other projects.

"When I came onto the project, there were already people involved," recalled Scott. "My first in-depth meetings about how sci-fi should be and how it should look were with Dan O'Bannon, who'd written the original screenplay with Ron Shusett." Scott storyboarded every scene of the film, to visualise how it would look for himself and as a tool to persuade the studio that the meagre $4.2 million budget was simply not enough to realise what he had in mind. So vibrant were the storyboards that Fox quickly doubled the budget, giving Scott $8.5 million. The storyboards, however, did not change the short shooting schedule, with filming set to run from July to October 1978, with some additional days for pick-ups and effects work towards the end of the year.

Setting out to explore an unfamiliar combination of science fiction and horror, two genres with which Scott admitted his unfamiliarity, the director was only too happy to remain open to the advice of those around him. Original writer Dan O'Bannon suggested that Scott take in a screening of Tobe Hooper's *The Texas Chainsaw Massacre*, then a cutting-edge horror film. Scott also took to repeatedly watching William Friedkin's frightfest *The Exorcist*. These films gave the director a feel for what was going on in contemporary horror cinema, while his experience of viewing *Star Wars* had shown him what could be achieved with clever special effects.

One of the keys to the success of *Alien* was undoubtedly the design employed. Scott inherited one designer from the Walter Hill version of the film: Ron Cobb, who'd worked on the Cantina sequence of *Star Wars* and who was to be behind the look of the spacecraft and the human technology in *Alien*. "O'Bannon introduced me to Ron Cobb, a brilliant visualiser of the genre with whom he had worked on *Dark Star* (1975, a comedic first draft of *Alien*)," remembered Scott. "Cobb seemed to have very realistic visions of both the far and near future, so I quickly decided that he would take a very important part in the making of the film. In fact, I brought both him and O'Bannon to England during the making of *Alien*, and he became a very important member of the art department [as a conceptual artist]. We based a lot of our interiors of the Nostromo on Cobb's visuals."

Ridley Scott realised one of his ambitions by hiring Moebius, the name under which *Heavy Metal* artist Jean Giraud worked, to deal with the design of the spacesuits and clothing worn by the main characters. Scott also hired an old friend from RSA, Michael Seymour. Seymour's role was to function as a traditional Production Designer, unifying the designs of Cobb, Giraud and Scott into a coherent whole. Only one element remained: who would design the title character, the other-worldly alien creature itself?

Scott was aware from even his limited exposure to science-fiction movies was that most of those which featured monsters or creatures tended to showcase terrible designs, men-in-suits or laughable creations. Scott knew he wanted something else altogether, something truly alien. To achieve that, he turned to Swiss designer and painter H R Giger. "Dan O'Bannon gave me a book of Giger's art one day," recalled Scott of his introduction to the artist's work. "I started flipping through it and nearly fell off my desk. I'd hit upon a particular painting (*Necronom IV*) with this frightening, truly unique creature in it. I took one look at the thing and said 'This is it! This is our beast!' That was that – I'd never been so sure of anything in my life."

The final piece of the *Alien* puzzle fell into place when Giger agreed to work on the film's non-human elements, including the alien creature, the eggs, facehugger and chestbuster, as well as the alien planet's surface and the derelict spacecraft the crew explore. Giger relocated to London's Shepperton Studios where *Alien* was filming and set up a construction workshop where he designed and built the full-size alien suit, which was worn in the film at various times by stuntman (and Hammer horror film veteran) the late Eddie 'Nosher' Powell and 7ft tall Nigerian art student Bolaji Badejo.

After the script and design elements, the other factor which contributed hugely to *Alien*'s success was the casting. It was an area in which Ridley Scott had always retained a special interest, from the leads down to the most minor walk-on part. Scott brought to the film an uneasy mixture of British (Ian Holm, John Hurt) and American actors (Tom Skerritt, Yaphet Kotto and Harry Dean Stanton). It was the female characters, however, who brought a unique twist to this unusual science-fiction film. Veronica Cartwright would later become better known for a recurring role on *The X-Files* TV show, while the lead role of Ripley went to an almost unknown, 28-year-old New York stage actress named Susan Weaver, better known as Sigourney Weaver. She was hired, said Scott, "because of Sigourney's own strength and intelligence. The idea of making the hero a heroine was truly a master stroke, because, of course, we fully expect Sigourney to be the first one to go, but this story is different. Sigourney was great because she has such presence and authority."

Unlike many science-fiction movies, Ridley Scott wanted to reflect some level of industrial reality in *Alien*. Most space films feature starship crews concentrated on the officer class – no-one ever pays any attention to the 'grunts', the below-decks guys who keep the ship going. This was something Scott set out to incorporate in his design. "The look was really meant to reflect the crew members who, I felt, should be like truck drivers in space," confirmed Scott. "Their jobs, which took them on several-year journeys through space, were to them a normal state of affairs. At the culmination of many long voyages, these ships look used, beat-up, covered in graffiti and uncomfortable. We certainly didn't design the Nostromo to look like a hotel."

This idea of being on journeys which took many years was reflected in the character interactions on board the ship, a part of the film which Scott emphasised. "I think the crew members of the Nostromo seem spirited only because of their argumentative nature, which is due to the fact they can probably no longer stand the sight of each other," the director said in a contemporary interview. "It wouldn't matter how it was worked out in the pre-voyage stage, when a computer probably determined the compatibility of the unit, like all crews in confined spaces, they'd get on one another's nerves and would be cutting each other's throats in six months time. We were told just enough about the characters, so we knew who the trouble-makers were and who the politicians were. It illustrated the class system of below and above decks."

Of course, the biggest factor in the success of *Alien* was the title creature itself. Careful thought went into the creation of the alien creature by the director: not just into how it would look, but how it would behave, what its motivations would be. "In relation to humans, the alien does seem to be indestructible," noted Scott of one of the problems he faced in making the story believable. "[The alien] does not fear anything. In fact, it is a supreme being. The kind of creature we came up with emerged from the logic of how it could reproduce itself. What gave us the cocoon concept was that insects will utilise others' bodies to be the hosts for their eggs. That's how the alien would use Kane and each of the crew members it kills. This explains why the alien doesn't kill everybody at once, but rather kills them off one by one: it wants to use each person as a separate host each time it has new eggs."

The pivotal scene in *Alien*, and the one most written about by contemporary critics and ever since, is the so-called 'chestbuster', when the 'baby' alien creature emerges from within the host, Kane, as the crew of the Nostromo sit down for a meal. For the first take of this key scene, Ridley Scott ensured that none of the cast, other than John Hurt as Kane, knew exactly what to expect. His aim was to capture genuine alarm from his actors. "I never showed them what was going to come out [of Kane]," claimed Scott. "We did it all on one take with four cameras running. All the effects were pre-set to go. It was all hand-held."

Playing Ripley, Sigourney Weaver confirmed: "I had seen the pictures [design concepts], but when the alien was born, it was a very funny day. In fact, Ridley wouldn't let any of us see it. As I walked on the set I remember everyone [on the crew] was wearing raincoats, which should have given me a hint that something horrible was going to happen. They never rehearsed it. John Hurt started screaming and because he's such a good actor, all I could think of was 'What's happening', not to John, but to Kane."

This was exactly the reaction Scott had wanted. Of course, reshoots and subsequent takes to capture different angles diluted the surprise impact, but nonetheless, the power of the final sequence is no doubt largely down to the shock of the other actors around that table, and most of that is genuine.

The shooting of *Alien* turned out to be an uncomfortable experience for almost everyone involved. For his part, Ridley Scott felt out of his depth: not because he couldn't cope with the requirements of the film, but because he couldn't cope with the demands of his studio bosses. Used to a certain amount of autonomy and freedom in making his commercials and *The Duellists*, he found it difficult to be answerable for every decision he made. The project was tightly budgeted and this, too, was a source of frustration for Scott.

The cast were none too happy either. Most complained of having thin roles, which ultimately resulted in them being alien fodder anyway. The film was low on dialogue and character development, high on impressive visuals and atmospheres – not a combination calculated to be particularly appealing or challenging to an actor.

Before release, Scott faced a battle with 20th Century Fox over the first cut of the movie. "The studio kept saying that nothing happens in the first 45 minutes," revealed Scott. "I said 'That's the whole point, but once it starts to happen, we'll have the audience.' It's revealing the world that these workers in space function in. Jerry Goldsmith's music maintains the tension."

That wasn't the only problem Scott faced with the money men behind the film: "There was an argument with the producers about the end," the director admitted. "They wanted it to end in the shuttle craft. I knew it couldn't end there, the story just wasn't right. The alien had to be in the shuttle craft. They said it was overkill, but in a movie like this you need overkill. I had the idea that we should really have an ending after the ending." For his part, Scott believed that the ending was so effective due to Sigourney Weaver. "For the last 17 minutes of the film or so there is no dialogue, except for Sigourney's utterances to herself. Everything is sustained by Sigourney and the sounds of the ship about to blow. Running backwards down the corridors was murder: it was just run, run, run and the thing's bouncing all over the place."

Reception: *Alien* was released by 20th Century Fox in the US on 25 May 1979, backed by an extensive advertising and merchandising campaign. The film was an undoubted hit, grossing $60 million in the US and $165 million worldwide by 2000. *Variety* noted of the film: '*Alien* is an old-fashioned scary movie set in a highly realistic future... director Ridley

Scott propels the emotions from one visual surprise – and horror – to the next.'

While critical reaction was generally favourable there were those who criticised the film for its violence. "Someone wrote that *Alien* was a manipulative piece of blood and guts movie-making with no redeeming features whatsoever," lamented Scott. "I knew I was making a vicious shocker, but I'd really wanted to back off the hard-core blood and gore. Excepting the 'chestbuster' sequence, *Alien* is almost totally devoid of blood and gore." Scott went on to complain that by concentrating on the viscera, critics had missed the contributions of Giger and Cobb to a unique environment, one that Scott felt marked his film out as more of a work of art than a mere 'vicious shocker'. He'd created a world, and all the critics could see was the gore. There was one more critical opinion which annoyed the director. "Critics have said you don't see enough of the alien, I think you see plenty of the alien," claimed Scott.

Facts And Figures:

• While developing the script, Scott brought his previous experience with *The Duellists* to bear in more than just practical ways. He turned to the works of Conrad for inspiration for names for the various spacecraft in the film. The main ship is the Nostromo, while the shuttle craft is Narcissus (both from Conrad titles). The name of the shadowy company behind the secret mission to retrieve the alien creature is Weyland-Yutani, again drawn from Conrad's *Heart Of Darkness*: they are the company who own the river boat which makes the fateful journey in the novella.

• The alien's habit of laying eggs in the stomach (which then burst out) is similar to the life cycle of the tsetse fly.

• A lawsuit by A E van Vogt, claiming plagiarism of his 1939 story *Discord In Scarlet* (which he had also incorporated in the 1950 novel *Voyage Of The Space Beagle*), was settled out of court.

• In the scene where Dallas, Kane and Lambert are leaving the ship, the actual actors walking past the Nostromo's landing struts are three children, two of whom were Scott's children (Jason and Luke) dressed in scaled-down spacesuits. "We put three children in miniature spacesuits – my two children and the cameraman's son – to make the landing legs look bigger," said Scott.

• Extra scenes were filmed but not included in the final cut. "There were many compromises, cuts, alterations and changes made before, during and after shooting," confirmed Scott. Some of the major scenes were: Ripley finds cocoons (one of which is Dallas) and destroys them with a flame thrower ("...When Ripley is running around on her own at the end of the film, she discovers that the alien has actually started a nest aboard the ship. The walls are covered with this thick, butter-like stuff, and Dallas, still alive, is attached to the wall in a cocoon-type of thing. Dallas says, 'Kill me!' and she incinerates the room" – Ridley Scott); an alternative death scene for Brett sees Ripley and Parker come across Brett being lifted from the ground; a scene that involves Parker, Ripley and Lambert trying to flush the alien out of the air lock ("What we called the decompression sequence. They've tracked the alien to an airlock and try to blow him out of the ship by throwing the doors open and having him sucked into space. But he's too quick for them. He does a flip backwards at the last moment. A little bit of acid is spewed on the airlock door, and eats right through it, breaking the seal even after they close the door. So the ship starts decompressing. We had to cut it in the end anyway. Too costly to shoot. Too much time. But it would have been killer." – Ridley Scott).

• Percy Edwards, who did the 'alien vocals,' was better known for his birdsong contributions to children's TV shows.

• The creature movements inside the first egg discovered are Ridley Scott's hands inside rubber gloves. The inside of the first facehugger was made of shellfish: oysters and clams. Scott prefers physical effects over costly computer-generated ones. "When you're forced to be inventive, the best comes out and it often works very well," noted the director.

Blade Runner (1982)

"It's too bad she won't live! But then again, who does?"

– Gaff, *Blade Runner*

Director: Ridley Scott, Writers: Philip K Dick (novel *Do Androids Dream Of Electric Sheep?*), Hampton Fancher & David Webb Peoples

Cast: Harrison Ford (Deckard), Rutger Hauer (Roy Batty), Sean Young (Rachael), Edward James Olmos (Gaff), M Emmet Walsh (Captain Bryant), Daryl Hannah (Pris), William Sanderson (J F Sebastian), Brion James (Leon), Joe Turkel (Tyrell), Joanna Cassidy (Zhora), James Hong (Chew), Morgan Paull (Holden)

Crew: Producers: Michael Deeley, Hampton Fancher (Executive), Brian Kelly (Executive), Jerry Perenchio (Co-Executive), Ivor Powell (Associate), Run Run Shaw (Associate), Bud Yorkin (Co-Executive); Music: Vangelis; Cinematography: Jordan Cronenweth; Editing: Marsha Nakashima; Production Design: Lawrence G Paull; Art Direction: David L Snyder;

Costumes: Jean Giraud (Uncredited), Michael Kaplan, Charles Knode; Visual Futurist: Syd Mead

Plot: Los Angeles, November 2019. A number of short-lived androids, replica humans or Nexus 6 'replicants,' have escaped the off-world colonies and returned to Earth. Led by Roy Batty, the replicants are returning to their maker, Dr Eldon Tyrell, to persuade him to extend their lives beyond their built-in four year span. Ex-'Blade Runner' cop, Rick Deckard is charged with 'retiring' the replicants... but could he be one of them?

Inspiration: Hollywood had all but ignored *The Duellists*. There was no way the movie-making establishment of America could ignore *Alien*, no matter how hard they tried. Although he was not a particularly big fan of the genre, Scott saw an opportunity to capitalise on his unexpected science-fiction success and even announced he wouldn't mind "becoming the John Ford of science fiction."

Thus an approach from Italian producer Dino De Laurentiis to Scott with another science-fiction property was very welcome by the rising-star director. Scott quickly signed up to direct a big-budget and ambitious film version of Frank Herbert's classic SF novel *Dune*. According to author Harlan Ellison, Scott made the "John Ford of science fiction" claim during a 1979 visit to his home to discuss Ellison writing the screenplay for *Dune*. "He was very nice about it when I told him I'd sooner spend my declining years vacationing on Devil's Island," claimed the cantankerous Ellison. "By 1980, the deal was dead. Scott went onto *Blade Runner*."

Scott wasn't the first director De Laurentiis had thrown at the project: Alejandro Jodorowsky, best known for the bizarre movies *El Topo* and *The Holy Mountain*, had previously tackled the project and failed to pull it together. Scott was drawn in by his desire to create worlds, and what bigger and better created world could there be than the one chronicled in obsessive detail in Herbert's series of novels.

During 1980 Scott had screenwriter Rudolph Wurlitzer working on a *Dune* script, but within six months the director had followed Jodorowsky and pulled out of the seemingly impossible to realise project. "I realised that *Dune* was going to take a lot more work – at least two and a half years worth. I didn't have the heart to attack that as my older brother, Frank, unexpectedly died of cancer while I was prepping the picture. That freaked me out, so I went to Dino and told him the *Dune* script was his. I concentrated on RSA for a while." The film was eventually made by David Lynch.

This understandable withdrawal from the hurly-burly world of film-making could not last long, however. Film-making was in Ridley Scott's blood and once he'd come to terms with his older brother's untimely demise, he was itching to get back behind a camera. "I got restless," Scott admitted of this period. "I realised that I needed even more activity to get my mind off my brother's death, so I started looking around for another film."

Development: Despite trying to capitalise on his science-fiction success with *Alien*, Scott was wary of repeating himself. He was keen to try out a new genre, something as different from *Alien* as that film had been from *The Duellists*. Instead, he found himself reading another science-fiction script entitled *Dangerous Days*, which he'd earlier rejected under the title of *Android* when he was prepping *Dune*. The script, by Hampton Fancher, was drawn from a Philip K Dick novel called *Do Androids Dream Of Electric Sheep?* and was presented to Scott by film producer Michael Deeley (*The Deer Hunter*).

Several attempts had been made to turn *Do Androids Dream Of Electric Sheep?* into a film before the 1980s. Martin Scorsese and Jay Cocks had shown an interest in the early 1970s, but had never formerly optioned the novel. Robert Jaffe, of Herb Jaffe Associates, did and wrote a script which Philip K Dick characterised as "along the lines of *Get Smart*. He turned it into a comedy spoof. It was so terribly done..." Jaffe let his option lapse in 1977, allowing Hampton Fancher, an ex-actor who'd been interested in adapting the book for some years, to snap up the rights. "It took nearly a year to write," said Fancher, "but when I took the script to Michael Deeley, he loved it."

Wary of another science-fiction script, Scott was nonetheless captivated by the moral content of the adaptation of Dick's novel. The idea of a state killer tracking down and murdering artificial people raised all sorts of questions the director was keen to explore, while the action possibilities of the police thriller form caught his visual imagination. It was, again, a chance for Scott to create a fully imagined world. "It was an extraordinary piece of work," noted Scott, "with marvellous design possibilities."

By February 1980 Scott had signed up to direct the film, by then retitled *Blade Runner*. The film began to fall apart. Budgeted at a mere $13 million, it was backed by Filmways, a minor studio that had emerged from the embers of Roger Corman's quick, low-budget production unit American-International Pictures. By December of 1980 Filmways had pulled out of *Blade Runner*, more concerned with its own financial problems than the funding of another movie. Production was due to begin in the following month. On top of that, Scott and screenwriter Hampton Fancher parted company after the director asked for rewrites to the screenplay which

Fancher didn't support. "Scott had some points that he wanted incorporated into the script," recalled Fancher. "[They were] ideas that I actively resisted. I was only interested in adding those things that I felt were worthwhile."

Scott brought in David Peoples, a screenwriter who'd been working with Tony Scott on an unmade project. A new production alliance had also been formed to fund the film, which consisted of Warner Brothers, cinema mogul Sir Run Run Shaw and Tandem Productions (a film and TV production company headed by Bud Yorkin). This unholy trio came up with a budget of $28 million for the film and a new shooting schedule, set to begin in March 1981 and run for 16 weeks, was drawn up.

Production: Ridley Scott's biggest challenge on *Blade Runner*, and the one which first attracted him to the film, was creating the future of Los Angeles in 2019. During his research, Scott came across a book entitled *Sentinel* which featured the imaginative future visions of artist Syd Mead. Mead had been a commercial artist for large American corporations who specialised in designs for cars and other transport, including early work on the Concorde supersonic jet. In his own way, Mead was doing on paper and with paint what Ridley Scott was doing on film: creating entire imaginary worlds. The team of Ridley Scott and Syd Mead was to be a marriage made in heaven.

Mead was first called upon to design the cars of *Blade Runner*, the flying 'spinners' which carried Deckard and his police colleagues. However, such was his obvious potential contribution to *Blade Runner* that Mead found his brief on the film expanded to include other items which defined *Blade Runner*'s future cityscape, including buildings, props and other vehicles. "I had a feeling that Syd would be able to place his vision within our film's time period," said Scott. For his part, Mead quickly adapted his sensibilities to the needs of the film: "I picked a general feeling of how they were going to slant the film in terms of scenery and lighting. Being able to help design the sets at least ensured that my cars would be seen in appropriate surroundings."

As well as Mead's influence, Scott turned to other films for inspiration. Prime among them was Fritz Lang's *Metropolis*, one of the earliest films to bring a futuristic cityscape successfully to the screen and a personal favourite of the director's.

As the look of *Blade Runner* was being locked down in pre-production and the 16-week Burbank, Los Angeles-based shoot loomed, Scott turned his attention to casting the film. Dustin Hoffman was his first choice for the role of detective Deckard, but Scott soon switched his attention to Harrison

Ford, who by 1980 was famous for his roles as Han Solo in *Star Wars* and Indiana Jones in *Raiders Of The Lost Ark*. Ford was a bankable name who would bring to the film the possibility of a big opening weekend, based on the draw of the star alone.

The other roles were quickly filled, with Sean Young being "perfect", according to Scott, for the part of Rachael; Daryl Hannah taking the role of Pris, the 'pleasure model' replicant and Dutch actor Rutger Hauer became Roy Batty, the driven, motivated leader of the band of rebelling replicants. All three were largely unknown at the time, but have all since gone on to build substantial, if variable, careers in Hollywood and beyond.

For all the criticism of Ridley Scott that he puts his visuals before his actors (after all, he did once claim: "There are certain moments where the background can be as important as the actor"), he was very careful in *Blade Runner* to work with the actors. "Before the film, I spent a little bit of time with the actors, finding a level and dimension for their characters. After a fair amount of discussion, the actor starts to key in on what he feels would be right for himself with what I want, and starts forming it himself along that route. It's almost like a sculpting process. You gradually build up the character as you go. I also find it useful to write out a biography of each character – it helps give the actor a direction."

In particular, the director wanted to ensure that those actors playing the replicants had a handle on their roles. "I spent time explaining to Rutger (Hauer) and Brion (James, as Leon) how the replicants were originally designed and what duties they would have performed. Almost like giving them a potted history of how science had developed up to this particular point and what uses had been found for what had essentially become a second-class generation. They started to key in on that and argue about it. As soon as you get an actor arguing about something, then you know you're getting somewhere."

If Scott thought the production was going to be easy, putting the funding troubles behind him and with a top-notch cast lined up, he was to be in for a surprise. A few days into filming, the director was clashing with the lighting director; two of the stars, Ford and Young, were barely speaking, while Ford turned on Scott, accusing the director of worrying too much about the special effects and not about the actors' performances. It was a feeling familiar to Ford from his work with George Lucas on *Star Wars* and *The Empire Strikes Back*. The actors felt overshadowed by the enormity of the film, by the sheer physically dominating nature of many of the sets and the demands of the special effects. Scott found himself having increasing problems with the cast and crew, mainly due to the director's demanding nature, his desire to get his vision of this future world perfect.

For his part, shooting a film in Los Angeles under American studio conditions was a new and strange experience. His work on *The Duellists* and *Alien* had been in Britain and France, well outwith the purview of American studio executives. He was used to having British crews who were almost as perfectionist as he was, and if they didn't always agree with the director, they at least recognised his place as the creative force behind the film. In many ways, Hollywood was a very foreign place for Ridley Scott. In particular, union restrictions, rules and regulations proved impenetrable to the director, although British technicians unions were just as hidebound in their enforcement of working practices. "I encountered a certain amount of frustration in dealing with certain Hollywood union regulations," admitted Scott.

Scott's biggest problem on *Blade Runner*, though, was to be with one of his own funding companies, Tandem Productions. They were the film's completion bond guarantors, with the power to take control of the film project if it went over the agreed budget. Almost as soon as Scott crossed the budget limit and spent more money than agreed, Tandem stepped in to take control of the film away from Scott and Deeley. As filming fell further behind, Bud Yorkin, unexpectedly, found himself running the show. For his part, Yorkin had a radically different vision for *Blade Runner* than the director, making for a series of clashes over the atmosphere of the film, the choice whether to have an explanatory voice-over narration and whether the ending should be upbeat and positive or downbeat and contemplative. These problems meant that many of the cast and crew were to see Ridley Scott in a negative light as he tried to finish the film while dealing with the interference of Tandem and Bud Yorkin. "I was questioned so often about everything I did or wanted to do," admitted Scott, "that the situation really pissed me off. That's when I became a screamer. I simply got fed up answering stupid questions."

After several, very negative test screening of work prints of the film, Scott lost two of the major battles. *Blade Runner* was saddled with a happy ending, infamously utilising out-takes from the Stanley Kubrick film *The Shining*, and also had a largely redundant monotone voice-over by Harrison Ford foisted upon it. The extensive voice-over was added to help people relate to Harrison Ford's character and make following the plot easier. After a draft by novelist-screenwriter Darryl Ponicsan was discarded, a TV veteran named Roland Kibbe got the job. As finally written, the voice-over met with universal scorn from the film-makers.

Both the voice-over and the tacked-on ending would later be removed by Scott for his 1992 'director's cut' of the film. Later DVD releases would see Scott even reinstating cut scenes which had become well known among *Blade Runner* fans, including a scene in which Deckard visits replicant interrogator Holden in hospital.

The tensions between director, producer and production company became so serious that during the editing process Scott and Deeley were actually fired from the production. Both found themselves quickly reinstated when Tandem realised that to get someone else to finish the film off would probably cost more in the long run.

For Scott, a successful score was almost as important to his films as the look. He'd been impressed with the work Jerry Goldsmith had done on *Alien*, but wanted to go in a different direction with *Blade Runner*. Scott saw the music adding significantly to the overall effect of the film. For this director, the music was not to be an afterthought, but a key part of the success of the final film. So Scott turned to Greek composer Vangelis.

Reception: Unfortunately for Scott in the short term it seemed as though his hard-fought battles over *Blade Runner* had not been worthwhile. The compromised first version of the film was released in the summer of 1982 and despite its fashionable SF tropes and the presence of Harrison Ford, *Blade Runner* flopped dismally at the box office. Word quickly spread that this was not another jaunty Harrison Ford action picture, but a dark, dystopic, downbeat thriller with no heroes and very little in the way of action sequences or feel-good quips.

Critical reaction was decidedly mixed. *The New York Times* called it 'muddled yet mesmerising'; *Time Magazine* said that the film, 'like its setting, is a beautiful, deadly organism that devours life'; and *The Los Angeles Times* complained: 'Blade crawler might be more like it.'

Audience bafflement and confusion about Ford's lack of heroics, and the fact that the $25 million film opened against the substantially more user-friendly *E.T.: The Extraterrestrial*, led to a paltry opening weekend take of $6 million and an overall gross of $14.5 million for its initial run.

However, despite its failure at the box office, *Blade Runner* did have its fans and champions even in 1982. They were a group which would grow over time and be instrumental in the growing critical acceptance of *Blade Runner* and the film's later commercial second life. Ten years later, in 1992, with the release of the revised Director's Cut of *Blade Runner*, the film received the welcome it deserved. According to *The Washington Post*: 'the film is great on every level: the poignant screenplay about man's futile quest for immortality; Scott's tremendous direction; the incredible, futuristic sets designed by Lawrence G Paull, Syd Mead and others; the phenomenal special effects; and the touching performances, especially from Hauer, a replicant fighting against the ebbing of his life. His swan song is one of the most touching in modern movie history.' Even *Entertainment Weekly* leapt on the bandwagon: '*Blade Runner* is a singular and enthralling experience. This is perhaps the only science-fiction film that can be called transcendental.'

That was yet to come, and in 1982 after the success of and acclaim for *Alien*, the failure of *Blade Runner* came as something of a shock to the director.

Is Deckard A Replicant? Over the years, *Blade Runner* gathered an ever-growing cult following. One of the issues which was endlessly discussed among *Blade Runner* fans was the status of Rick Deckard. At the beginning of the film Bryant tells Deckard that six replicants (three male, three female) have arrived on Earth, but we only ever see five accounted for: Roy Batty, Leon, Pris, Zhora and one other identified in dialogue as having been terminated already ("one of them got fried trying to get into the Tyrell building" – Bryant). Could Deckard himself have been the missing sixth replicant? The evidence against is that in the original work print of the film, the dialogue from Bryant was recorded to specify that two replicants were fried breaking into the Tyrell building.

There is other evidence, though. In one moment in the original 1982 release, Deckard's eyes are seen to glow red briefly and in the background, just like Batty's. That subtle clue was all that was left in the film, but the film-makers had debated the subject among themselves. Hampton Fancher's original script was quite explicit: "I ended the film with Deckard's hand cramping up, just like Batty's. I wanted the audience to walk away thinking, 'Is Deckard like Batty?'"

David Peoples' original ending had Deckard musing on the nature of humanity in voice-over, but his words were misinterpreted by Scott to mean that Deckard was a replicant. "The script read: 'In my own modest way, I was a combat model. Roy Batty was my late brother.' He was supposed to be realising that, on a human level, they weren't so different. I think Ridley misinterpreted me, because he started announcing: 'Deckard's a replicant! What brilliance!'"

In the original 1982 cut of the film, Deckard's ex-colleague Gaff leaves a tinfoil unicorn at Deckard's apartment. It's a moment that had no meaning, until the 1992 Director's Cut rerelease. Scott inserted a scene (using material from his next movie *Legend*) where Deckard dreams of a unicorn, but doesn't react as though the creature were mythical or the dream in any way out of the ordinary. How could Gaff know of Deckard's dreams, unless it was an implanted memory, like Rachael's? Therefore, Deckard is a replicant.

The idea actually dated back to Philip K Dick's original novel, where Deckard's own status as a possible android is questioned. "The purpose of this story as I saw it," said Dick, "was that in his job of hunting and killing these replicants, Deckard becomes progressively dehumanised. At the same time, the replicants are being perceived as becoming more human. Finally, Deckard must question what he is doing, and really what is the essential difference between him and them? And, to take it one step further, who is he if there is no real difference?"

However, Deckard actor Harrison Ford was against the idea of the hero being just like the villains of the film. "There was always some contest between Ridley and I about whether or not the character was a replicant," said Ford. "I insisted the character could not be a replicant, because then the audience would have no emotional representative on the screen. It would be filled with people who are not human, and I thought the audience deserved at least one. I was aware that Ridley did not fully agree with me while we were making the film. He kept slipping in little details which indicated that I was one of them, but I never agreed with him."

The for and against arguments were laid to rest in the year 2000 in a BBC documentary on the film, *On The Edge Of Blade Runner*, in which Ridley Scott confirms: "He's a replicant."

Facts And Figures:

• The chess game between Tyrell and Sebastian uses the conclusion of a game played between Anderssen and Kieseritzky, in London in 1851. It is considered one of the most brilliant games ever played, and is universally known as 'The Immortal Game'.

• The following definition appears in the *Blade Runner* script and the Marvel Comics adaptation of the film, and on screen for the first Denver/Dallas sneak preview: 'android (an'droid) n, Gk. humanoid automation. robot. 1. early version utilised for work too boring, dangerous or unpleasant for humans. 2. second generation bio-engineered. Electronic relay units and positronic brains. Used in space to explore inhospitable environments. 3. third generation synthogenetic. Replicant, constructed of skin/flesh culture. Selected enogenic transfer conversion. Capable of self-perpetuating thought. Paraphysical abilities. Developed for emigration programme.'

• There are at least five different versions of *Blade Runner* known to exist, all slightly different: US Denver/Dallas Sneak Preview/Work print

(113 minutes, 1982, replicant definition, no voice-over, bleak ending); US San Diego Sneak Preview (115 minutes, 1982, minor extra scenes, happy ending); US Theatrical Release (115 minutes, 1982); European Theatrical Release (117 minutes, 1982, extra violence); and The Director's Cut (117 minutes, 1992, no voice-over, unicorn dream added, new digital soundtrack, bleak ending).

• Roy Batty's death speech ("all those moments will be lost in time, like tears in rain. Time to die") was ad libbed by actor Rutger Hauer on the day of shooting.

• Eye symbolism is rampant in *Blade Runner*: the eye in the opening shots; replicants' eyes glow; Tyrell has huge glasses to make his eyes bigger; eyes are used in the Voight-Kampf empathy test; there's 'Chew's Eye World' where Chew and Leon both handle the eyes; Leon tries to stick his fingers in Deckard's eyes; Batty plays with the glass-encased eyes in Sebastian's apartment; Batty sticks his thumbs in Tyrell's eyes; Pris rolls her eyes to show only the whites; the owl's large eyes are shown frequently.

• The *Blade Runner* story was continued in a series of novels by Dick's protégé K W Jeter.

• Some historical Los Angeles locations are featured in *Blade Runner*. The front of the Ennis Brown house in the Los Feliz area is seen in the film as the entrance to Harrison Ford's apartment building, a huge condominium complex, hundreds of stories high. It was designed in 1924 by Frank Lloyd Wright in a Mayan block motif. The building, the most monumental of Wright's western experimental work, has featured in many movies. The Bradbury Building, built in 1893, was preserved on film by *Blade Runner*. In one scene, Ford traces Hauer to the ornate edifice for the final showdown. In another, industrial designer J F Sebastian (William J Sanderson) discovers street waif Pris (Daryl Hannah) and takes her into his apartment. The Bradbury Building, at 304 S Broadway, was previously featured in Harlan Ellison's 'Demon With a Glass Hand' episode for *The Outer Limits* and later appeared in the Jack Nicholson film *Wolf*. Actors Rutger Hauer, Brion James and James Hong worked for two days amid icicles at US Growers Cold Storage, Inc, also in LA.

• When Gaff picks up Deckard in his spinner, the launch sequence on the computer is the same one used in Scott's *Alien*, where the escape pod separates from the Mothership. The black-and-white display of the Voight-Kampf machine was also previously seen as a wall display in *Alien*. When Deckard enters his apartment at the end, the background hum is also the same distinctive hum as in parts of *Alien*.

- Fans have speculated on the *Blade Runner* curse, pointing out that key companies advertised in the film have gone out of business in the years since 1982, including Pan Am, Atari, Bell Telephone (broken up by the US Government), and Cusinart. Even Coca Cola (still going strong) took a tumble when it released 'new formula' coke to a disastrous reception soon after *Blade Runner* was released.

Legend (1985)

"Beneath the skin we are already one."

– Darkness to Lili, *Legend*.

Director: Ridley Scott, Writer: William Hjortsberg

Cast: Tom Cruise (Jack), Mia Sara (Princess Lili), Tim Curry (Darkness), David Bennent (Gump), Alice Playten (Blix), Billy Barty (Screwball), Cork Hubbert (Brown Tom), Peter O'Farrell (Pox), Kiran Shah (Blunder), Annabelle Lanyon (Oona), Robert Picardo (Meg Mucklebones), Tina Martin (Nell), Ian Longmur (Demon Cook), Mike Crane (Demon Cook), Liz Gilbert (Dancing Black Dress), Eddie Powell (Mummified Guard)

Crew: Producers: Tim Hampton (Co-Producer), Arnon Milchan; Original Music: Jerry Goldsmith (European Version), Tangerine Dream (US Version); Cinematography: Alex Thomson; Editing: Terry Rawlings; Production Design: Leslie Dilley, Assheton Gorton; Costume Design: Charles Knode; Make-Up Department: Rob Bottin (Special Make-Up Effects), Lois Burwell (Make-Up Artist), Nick Dudman (Prosthetic Make-Up Artist), Peter Robb-King (Make-Up Artist)

Plot: At its heart the storyline of *Legend* was very simple: a conflict between good and evil, represented by Lili and Jack and the Lord of Darkness. Darkness plans to eliminate the last of the unicorns, causing eternal night to fall on the land. Lili is kidnapped by the demonic creature, prompting Jack of the forest to embark on a rescue mission to recover both the Princess and the unicorn, thereby restoring peace to the forest.

Inspiration: At the time of its release, *Blade Runner* appeared to be Ridley Scott's first high-profile failure. With *The Duellists*, Scott had succeeded in the limited way that his low budget allowed in recreating a historical reality. He'd used cinematic slight of hand to maximise his limited resources. Similarly, with *Alien*, he'd succeeded in creating a unique world, but it was one confined within one ship. With *Blade Runner* he'd gone for the big one. He'd attempted to realise on film a whole future city and society, again on a limited budget and with limited resources and with limited cooperation from those involved on the film. Although in time *Blade Runner* would come to be regarded first as a cult movie and later as a legitimate cinematic masterpiece, in 1982 it was a first for Ridley Scott: a critical and commercial failure.

That failure gave Scott pause for thought. The creation of *Blade Runner* had taken its toll on the director. He'd had to fight every inch of the way, against producers, financiers and even stars who, it appeared, did not share his vision. Even worse, upon release the film had been met with either indifference or critical complaints about the visuals winning out over the acting or the characters. The effort in achieving his vision didn't seem worthwhile to Scott. Perhaps, he felt, he'd be better off returning to London to run RSA, his still-thriving advertising business. That was a world he understood, one in which he could function, unlike – it seemed – in Hollywood. "I'd been very disappointed with the initial impact of *Blade Runner*," admitted Scott. "I thought I'd done a rather unique picture, but it wasn't received well, and while I was making it, I'd sometimes felt completely on my own."

At heart, though, Scott was a film-maker. That much was clear from his next project, an advert for the then brand new Apple Macintosh computer which, in terms of its visuals, put many big-budget Hollywood films to shame. Advertising agency Chiat/Day approached Scott's RSA to create a film for the Macintosh computer to run in a prime ad break during the January 1984 Superbowl. With that guaranteed audience and the attraction of creating a riff on Orwell's novel *1984*, Scott could do nothing other than direct the two-minute slot himself.

The ad could be a modern version of *Metropolis*, the film Scott admired so much and had influenced some aspects of *Blade Runner*. Featuring shambling, shaven-headed downtrodden workers, the ad featured the classic 'Big Brother' image exhorting the workers to do more, work harder and not to think. Enter a female athlete wielding an Olympic hammer, pursued by the forces of oppression. As the hammer strikes the giant, dominating screen, it shatters followed by the promise that thanks to the Apple Macintosh, the actual year 1984 would not be like Orwell's novel.

Scott returned to Shepperton Studios in London to shoot the commercial, using the same stages where he'd filmed *Alien* several years before. Although the ad was only broadcast in America once, it has been well remembered such was its impact. According to *The Guinness Book Of Records*, which claims that the ad was one of American TV's most expensive: "Recall [of the ad] among viewers is so high that it is believed to be one of the most cost-effective commercials ever made."

It wasn't long after *Blade Runner* when Ridley Scott decided he'd better get back in the movie game. This time, he'd create his own project, do all he could to retain control of it and beat the Hollywood industry on its own terms. At least, those were Scott's aims when he embarked on the fraught making of *Legend*.

Development: "In 1982, I still wanted to do a Medieval fantasy," claimed Scott, recalling his previous attempt to make a film version of *Tristan And Isolde*. "[I wanted a film] that would have a 'no time, no place' feel. It would lie somewhere between Cocteau's *Beauty And The Beast* and the 1935 Hollywood version of *A Midsummer Night's Dream* with James Cagney. I wanted to make something lighter, since my first three films were rather intense and heavy."

Looking at novels as source material for this new film, Scott came across the works of William Hjortsberg, author of the 1978 occult thriller *Falling Angel* (filmed in 1987 by Alan Parker as *Angel Heart*). Scott contacted Hjortsberg with a view to having him work on a script for this 'fairy-tale' based movie. Little did Hjortsberg realise he'd be involved in 15 drafts of the script over a four-year period.

Discussions between Scott and Hjortsberg centred around the themes and atmospheres the director wanted to pervade what he intended to be a timeless family movie about a clash between good and evil. "It's not a film of the future, or the past," said Scott. "It is not even a story of now. The conflict between darkness and light has been with us since the creation... and will remain with us throughout eternity." Among the inspirations the pair hoped to draw on were fairy tales like *Sleeping Beauty* as well as the darker stories of the Brothers Grimm and even *The Bible*. Scott wanted to deal with themes of temptation, sin, forgiveness and redemption.

In fact, Hjortsberg went too far to the dark side for his first draft, which was more disturbing and nightmarish than Scott anticipated, even featuring an intimate scene between heroine Lili and the Lord of Darkness, the film's devil figure. It was not the stuff of family entertainment. Scott wanted a subtler approach to the themes he sought to portray, so Hjortsberg went off to revise the script. Finally, the pair arrived at a working script that both agreed could be a basis to start production.

Production: Once more, creating the world of *Legend* (or *Legend Of Darkness* as it was initially called) would take its toll on the director. Scott needed a mythical forest, so began scouting locations in northern California, hoping the giant Redwoods would provide what he was looking for. It was not to be, and Scott instead settled for shooting on a soundstage at England's Pinewood Studios, just outside London. Here, Scott could control the film much more than out in nature. Scott recruited Assheton Gorton as the film's Production Designer and charged him with the task of bringing the forest of *Legend* to life.

Storyboards brought the film alive for Scott before a single frame of film was shot. The artistic influences on the visualisation of the film included the fairy-tale work of Arthur Rackham, the goblin and fairy illustrations of artist Brian Froud (later used again in *Labyrinth*) and the work of William Blake. Artists Sherman Labby and Martin Asbury created three volumes of storyboards, running to 411 pages, much more than would ever be used for a 90-minute film.

For *Legend* Scott set out to use a relatively unknown cast in order to foreground the magical elements of the film. He was worried that well-known actors would distract from the magical world he was hoping to create on screen. For the naive but heroic Jack O'Lantern, Scott signed up a young Tom Cruise, whose performances in *Taps* (1981) and *Risky Business* (1983) had caught the director's attention. Scott screened the 1970 François Truffaut film *The Wild Child* to show Cruise the kind of character he wanted Jack to be. Mia Sara, as Lili who has to face being seduced by Darkness, was cast "straight out of drama school," according to Scott. Assorted goblins and woodland creatures were played by David Bennent (who'd featured in Volker Schlöndorff's *The Tin Drum*, 1979), Alice Playten, Billy Barty, Annabelle Layton and Robert Picardo. Picardo played Meg Mucklebones, the swamp creature. He was well used to acting under masks thanks to his appearances in the early films of Joe Dante and is now better known as the holographic Doctor on the seven seasons of *Star Trek: Voyager*.

One role remained uncast: the part of Darkness, the demon of the tale. This was the (literally) big role in the film, one which depended on the right performer to pull it off. Scott knew that it would be very easy for the film to be laughable if the main villain of the piece was not realised properly, in the same way that *Alien* would have failed had the creature been badly realised. "I remembered Tim Curry from *The Rocky Horror Picture Show*," said Scott. "I wanted a performer who could get away with Darkness' unique blend of menace and humour." Curry faced hours in the make-up chair every day of filming as make-up and special-effects artist Rob Bottin, who was behind the eye-popping special effects of the remake of *The Thing* (1982), turned the actor into a hugely horned, red-skinned, cloven-hoofed demon. "He has a touch of genius," said Scott of Bottin.

On 23 March 1984 principal photography began on *Legend* and lasted a total of 21 weeks. The film was being helmed by a director who was not as confident of his abilities as he had once been. *Blade Runner* had been a nightmare project for Ridley Scott, and although his successful Apple Macintosh ad spot had gone some way to restoring his self-confidence, the enormity of *Legend* was on his mind as the camera turned over that first day. "My confidence was a little uneven," admitted Scott. "Making *Legend* was actually rather scary."

Most of the shooting on the film took place within the confines of the so-called 007 soundstage at Paramount, Britain's biggest studio space built especially for the James Bond movies. There the forest where *Legend* was set had been erected. Apart from a brief location shoot in Florida (an underwater sequence which sees Jack retrieve Lili's ring), everything was shot at Pinewood.

It was something of a disaster, then, when on 27 June 1984 the James Bond soundstage burned to the ground, destroying *Legend*'s huge (and hugely expensive) forest set. Scott was on site when the fire happened, but he could do little but stand and watch as firefighters fought in vain to save the stage. The source of the fire was tracked to a build-up of gas fumes due to poor ventilation on the soundstage which were ignited by a freak electrical spark. Scott had three weeks of filming remaining, but no studio set to film on.

Despite this setback, the film actually only lost three days of shooting, according to Scott, as Production Designer Assheton Gorton saved the day by speeding up work on the film's other sets, allowing the production to be remounted quickly. Elements of the film were lost, however. Gorton lamented the fact that they'd lost the master set-ups for "an amazing tracking shot that everyone was excited about..." Scott saw the disaster during production as something of a bad omen, recalling something of the production problems he'd suffered during *Blade Runner*.

These thoughts returned to Scott after the film was completed and was undergoing test screenings. The 113-minute cut of the film shown to select audiences to gauge reaction was almost uniformly negatively received. Scott was shaken by the poor response to the movie and fearing another *Blade Runner*-style commercial failure, he set about re-editing the movie.

This process resulted in two versions of *Legend*: a domestic US edit at 89 minutes and featuring an electronic score by Tangerine Dream and a longer 94-minute European and international version which featured an edited version of the original Jerry Goldsmith score. The change to the music score and some of the edits on the US version of the film were dictated by Universal, the film's US distributor. In an effort to avoid another *Blade Runner*-type stand-off between the director and the studio, Scott decided to comply with the changes. He hoped his longer European version of the film retained enough of his original intention to attract an audience overseas. "As far as I'm concerned, we had an amazing piece of work, and then we were told to make *Legend* much shorter," said editor Terry Rawlings. "It lost something and the audience will never know what that was." Composer Jerry Goldsmith, whose score suffered immensely in the process, agreed: "I think the real victim is the picture. The entire concept of the film has been totally changed."

Scott even changed the ending of the film from that he'd originally intended, telling an interviewer in *Le Monde*: "At the end of the film, when the princess awakens and the young lovers talk and embrace, there is a certain voyeurism, a thread of sexuality and still more of innocence, for the sexuality comes from Lord Darkness. The princess removes the ring from her finger and gives it to him saying: 'I want you to accept this before I leave.' She runs into the forest, turns around and waves, beaming with happiness. We see him alone, standing, contemplating his domain, the forest. Slowly, he begins to cry. I loved that moment, like a suspension of innocence. The immediate reaction is: What, he's not carrying off the girl? Obviously he will have the girl, but a little later – the next day perhaps. Their relationship is going to develop. I like this ambiguity. For me, this is a completely optimistic ending."

Scott blamed the American habit of previewing films and letting unrepresentative, somewhat fickle audiences dictate film-makers creative choices. "The more you preview, the more dangerous it gets," claimed the director. "You then start to whittle away at stuff you shouldn't whittle away at. I cut a lot of interesting stuff out of *Legend* that I'm now sorry is gone. Don't forget, I was also very insecure after *Blade Runner*. [On that film] I felt sure I really had something, then watched it fail. What happened on *Legend* was definitely the result of my own crisis of confidence..."

Reception: Originally scheduled for American release in June 1985, *Legend* finally made its bow after re-editing in May 1986, missing a rescheduled release slot in November 1985. The film was lucky to run more than a couple of weeks in cinemas as it failed to find an appreciative audience. Critical reaction was not good and despite what he'd hoped Scott's own editing of the film had made matters worse.

The view of Roger Ebert of *The Chicago Sun-Times* was typical of critics, praising Scott's visual sense, but finding the movie to be unengaging. 'Let it be said that *Legend* is an impressive technical achievement,' wrote

47

Ebert. 'Scott is a perfectionist who takes infinite pains to make things look right, but performances tend to get lost in productions like this. Despite all its sound and fury, *Legend* is a movie I didn't care very much about. All of the special effects in the world, and all of the great make-up, can't save a movie that has no clear idea of its own mission and no joy in its own accomplishment.'

Ridley Scott was forced by the box-office numbers to admit that the re-editing hadn't worked: "The film didn't do that great in Europe either. All the re-editing and score changes were really for nothing..." However, like *Blade Runner*, *Legend* would be rediscovered by a dedicated and loyal fan base who did much to provoke a critical re-evaluation of what is perhaps Ridley Scott's most flawed film, his biggest but most ambitious failure to realise a complete fantasy land on film. The film took a meagre $15.5 million at the US box office.

At the time, though, Ridley Scott's state of mind after his second failure in a row was not healthy. "I kind of lost it," Scott admitted. It seemed that Ridley Scott's career as an A-list movie-maker had come to a premature end before it had really started.

Facts And Figures:

• There are three versions of *Legend* widely known about: the US cinema release (89 minutes, with the Tangerine Dream score), the European cinema release (94 minutes, with the Jerry Goldsmith score) and a television version broadcast by PBS in the US (94 minutes, with a mixed score). There are other 'working' versions of the film said to exist, including a 140-minute work print, Ridley Scott's first cut of 125 minutes and later edits following the edicts from Universal of 113 minutes and 98 minutes. There are too many differences between each version to list them all here, but if you want an exhaustive list, check out the *Legend* FAQ (Frequently Asked Questions) website at www.figmentfly.com/legend/index.shtml.

• The score composed by Jerry Goldsmith for *Legend* was 80 minutes long and was recorded in London with a full orchestra and chorus, augmented with synthesisers. Scott called it "exactly what was required [for the film]." Goldsmith considered the score to be "one of the best soundtracks I've ever done," and remains his favourite, making it all the sadder that the work was replaced by the Tangerine Dream score by Universal in an effort to appeal to the 'youth market'. Tangerine Dream had previously contributed to the score for the Tom Cruise movie *Risky Business*, a fact which probably contributed to their involvement in re-scoring *Legend*.

• To add insult to injury (or vice versa) both the session master tape and the entire written score (including the composer's sketches, orchestrations and instrumental parts) were 'misplaced' and apparently lost for good. "They disappeared into thin air," said Goldsmith in an interview with *The Cue Sheet* magazine of the tapes and music score. "It's very weird. Nobody knows where they are. I'm upset about it. Everything has disappeared: the 48-track is gone, there's nothing else left." Thankfully, recording engineer Mike Ross had preserved a two-track digital copy of the session master tapes, used for the 1992 expanded CD reissue of Goldsmith's original score.

• Like the missing Replicant in *Blade Runner*, *Legend* has its own 'missing goblin' mystery. The character of Tic, played by Mike Edmonds, was cut from all released versions of *Legend*, but can be seen briefly in one scene of the European release of the film. As the goblins are chasing the unicorns, it is possible to discern four goblins rather than three chasing the mythical animals.

• Ridley Scott feels it is unlikely that there will ever be a restored Director's Cut of *Legend* as there was for *Blade Runner*. "There was always a regret that because we didn't preview well, we cut out almost half an hour," confirmed Scott. "I'm always passionate about my work, but I doubt there will be a director's cut. I am curious how it would do if it [the first cut of *Legend*] were released today."

4. The Crime Trilogy

Someone To Watch Over Me (1987)

"Is it love, Mike? I hope so – I want it to be worth it for your sake."
– Lt. Garber, *Someone To Watch Over Me*

Director: Ridley Scott, Writers: Howard Franklin, Danilo Bach (Uncredited), David Seltzer (Uncredited)

Cast: Tom Berenger (Mike Keegan), Mimi Rogers (Claire Gregory), Lorraine Bracco (Ellie Keegan), Jerry Orbach (Lt. Garber), John Rubinstein (Neil Steinhart), Andreas Katsulas (Joey Venza), Tony DiBenedetto (T J), James E Moriarty (Koontz)

Crew: Producers: Thierry de Ganay, Mimi Polk (Associate), Harold Schneider, Ridley Scott (Executive); Music: Michael Kamen, Vangelis, Léo Delibes (from 'Lakmé'), Antonio Vivaldi; Cinematography: Steven B Poster; Editing: Claire Simpson; Production Design: James D Bissell; Art Direction: Christopher Burian-Mohr, Jay Moore; Costume Design: Colleen Atwood

Plot: Flashy cop thriller in which New York socialite Claire Gregory witnesses a murder and is then threatened by the killer, Joey Venza. Assigned to protect Gregory is Queens' cop Mike Keegan. He's soon involved with the woman he's charged with protecting...

Inspiration: The detailed worlds which Ridley Scott created in *Alien, Blade Runner* and *Legend* clearly fulfilled his own ambitions for his filmmaking, but were to prove something of a cinematic albatross as his career as a 'Hollywood' director moved into a new phase. With the possible exception of *1492: Conquest Of Paradise*, Scott's films would not feature the same depth of 'created worlds' until the historical blockbuster *Gladiator* (2000).

The making of *Blade Runner* and *Legend* had taken their toll on the director, both personally and professionally. For his fourth film, Ridley Scott turned away from the complex science-fiction and fantasy epics which had occupied him for almost 10 years and began work on what the director himself dubbed a "normal" film. For Scott, after the problems he'd had on his two previous films, the prospect of making a contemporary thriller was highly attractive. "I figured I'd better go down the road of being normal after what had happened with *Blade Runner* and *Legend*." The process of trying to be 'normal' would prove one thing to Ridley Scott:

"I've discovered that I shouldn't try to be conventional. Not many people can do great oddball stuff."

Rather than seeking out the project, *Someone To Watch Over Me* fell into Scott's lap. At a dinner party in 1985, screenwriter Howard Franklin found himself pitching a storyline to Scott, not expecting the director to do anything with it. At the time Scott was working on a project then entitled *Johnny Utah*, which was stalled in script development, much to the director's disenchantment. The film was later made in 1991 by director Kathryn Bigelow under the title *Point Break*, starring Keanu Reeves and Patrick Swayze. To Franklin's astonishment, the director loved the story the writer had outlined and the pair set about developing the bare bones of the plot into a fully-fledged screenplay.

Scott was attracted to the story as much by the emotional dilemma faced by the central character as by the straightforward thriller elements. There was also the undercurrent of class conflict - a subtext of *Alien* - to explore. "I liked the contrast and coming together of the two main characters different social classes," noted Scott. "Everyone says there's no class system in the United States and that's rubbish."

Although he has a family and is happily married to the straight-talking Ellie (Lorraine Bracco), Keegan finds himself slowly drawn into Gregory's life and socialite lifestyle after first disparaging her upper-class ways. For her part, Gregory is attracted to her protector and has little regard for his family background. "What attracted me to Howard Franklin's idea was the situation of a good marriage having this intrusive element, a very tempting one, unexpectedly entering the equation," said Scott. "The Berenger character isn't looking for an affair, but both he and Mimi Rogers are thrown together in this high-pressure situation."

Production: Scott called on Tom Berenger for the part of the cop drawn into temptation. He'd seen the actor's contrasting performances in *The Big Chill* and Oliver Stone's *Platoon*. He believed that Berenger had the right adaptability to take on the part of the straightforward cop who finds himself drawn into a world he doesn't understand, but nonetheless finds fascinating. For the villain of the piece, Scott cast Andreas Katsulas, a stage actor then beginning to make inroads into film and television. He would later play the infamous one-armed man in the film version of *The Fugitive* and a regular role on the acclaimed science-fiction TV series *Babylon 5*. For the part of Keegan's wife Scott found a new acting talent in Lorraine Bracco who made her acting debut in the film. For Scott's money the character of Ellie and actress Bracco were ideally matched. "What you see in the film is exactly who Lorraine is," claimed the director. Bracco would later go on to feature in films such as *Goodfellas, The Basketball Diaries* and the critically acclaimed TV series *The Sopranos*.

Someone To Watch Over Me was shot during the autumn of 1986 on location in Manhattan, Queens and Los Angeles. Inevitably, it was often cheaper and quicker to recreate supposed New York locations in Los Angeles than to actually film on the busy streets and in the buildings of the metropolis. Gregory's townhouse was created at the Sony Pictures Studio in Culver City, while the opening party scene was filmed in LA's historic Mayan Theatre. Even more unusual locations were used, such as the swimming pool inside the Queen Mary, an out-of-service liner in Long Beach, which featured as a location at the climax of the film.

The shoot took 11 weeks, but compared to Scott's recent experiences, *Someone To Watch Over Me* was a relatively easy film to make. It was shot on location and in studios in fairly normal and realistic environments. There were no alien creatures, no fantastic futuristic sets and no unicorns. Looking at Scott's career as a whole, this was to prove to be the film he made with least effort – and the critical reaction seemed to appreciate that.

Opening Shot: Perhaps the most impressive element of *Someone To Watch Over Me* is the single take opening shot, a swooping, majestic shot which begins at the famous Chrysler Building before crossing the Hudson River and coming to rest at the down-to-earth home of Ellie and Mike Keegan. The shot was completed by Scott personally, from a helicopter, during the film's post-production period. A huge fan of the Chrysler Building for its unique design, Scott was determined to include it in the film, just as he'd been determined to utilise the equally distinctive Bradbury Building in *Blade Runner*.

Release: Upon release, *Someone To Watch Over Me* grossed just over $10 million in the US, making it one of Ridley Scott's lowest earning films. His attempts to break into the mainstream thriller arena had fallen on stony ground, as audiences stayed away from a film populated by c-level stars and which encouraged the 'nice visuals, shame about the acting and plot' critical reaction which often haunted Scott's movies. In fact, for Rita Kempley, writing in *The Washington Post*, Ridley Scott as a director was simply too good for material like *Someone To Watch Over Me*. 'With its stunning cityscapes and Chanel-ad surreality, *Someone To Watch Over Me* shows off director Ridley Scott's extraordinary visual artistry,' she wrote in praise of the director, before concluding: 'A lesser director might have handled this modest proposal better, might have made less of a production of what is a rather plain action drama.' For Roger Ebert, writing in *The Chicago Sun-Times*, *Someone To Watch Over Me* was passionless in more ways than one: 'The movie's high-tech sex scenes are done with all the cinematic technical support the director, Ridley Scott, can muster, but they're dead because they contain only sex, not passion.'

This poor critical reaction was not enough to throw Ridley Scott. "We nailed a good story in *Someone To Watch Over Me*," claimed Scott. Audiences, however, just didn't care. Unlike the more engaging though flawed films like *Blade Runner* and *Legend*, *Someone To Watch Over Me* has not excited the same interest over the longer term. Scott seems to have gone crazy with the lighting, thinking he's making an 1980s pop promo, while the storyline is a dry-run for the Kevin Costner-Whitney Houston movie *The Bodyguard*. *Someone To Watch Over Me* is simply a flash, empty thriller which is typical of so much Hollywood cinema of the 1980s and, unfortunately, one of Ridley Scott's least significant works.

Facts And Figures:

• The shoot-out in the mirrored dressing room is a homage to the Orson Welles film *The Lady From Shanghai* which climaxes with a shoot-out in a Hall of Mirrors.

Black Rain (1989)

"All America is good for anymore is movies and music. We make the machines, we build the future, we won the peace!"

– Osaka's police chief, *Black Rain*.

Director: Ridley Scott, Writers: Craig Bolotin & Warren Lewis

Cast: Michael Douglas (Nick Conklin), Andy Garcia (Charlie Vincent), Ken Takakura (Masahiro Matsumoto), Kate Capshaw (Joyce), Yusaku Matsuda (Kogi Sato), Tomisaburo Wakayama (Sugai), Shigeru Kouyama (Superintendent Ohashi), Vondie Curtis-Hall (Detective), Guts Ishimatsu (Katayama)

Crew: Producers: Craig Bolotin (Executive), Stanley R Jaffe, Julie Kirkham (Executive), Sherry Lansing, Alan Poul (Associate); Music: Hans Zimmer; Cinematography: Jan de Bont; Editing: Tom Rolf; Production Design: Norris Spencer; Art Direction: John Jay Moore, Kazuo Takenaka, Herman F Zimmerman; Costume Design: Ellen Mirojnick

Plot: A corrupt New York cop learns the value of honour from a Japanese cop, who in turn learns from the American the importance of individuality. Charged with escorting a Japanese gangster, Sato, a member of the yakuza in American custody, back to police custody in Japan, Nick Conklin and clean young cop Charlie Vincent pursue the escaped prisoner through a rarely seen side of Japan seething with mob violence, prostitution, homelessness and near-peasant rural life.

Inspiration: Ridley Scott had found directing *Someone To Watch Over Me* to be something of a relief after the trials and tribulations on *Blade Runner* and *Legend*. He so enjoyed directing a "normal" film, he decided to do it again when the opportunity arose, despite the poor critical reaction and box office of *Someone To Watch Over Me*. His opportunity came when Dutch director Paul Verhoeven (*Robocop*), who had been tapped by Paramount to tackle the culture clash cop movie *Black Rain,* pulled out deciding that he didn't have the touch required to carry the film off.

Having seen the stylish thriller *Someone To Watch Over Me*, Paramount executives Sherry Lansing and Stanley Jaffe approached Ridley Scott. "It was the first time I did a film as a director for hire," admitted Scott. "I was only directing *Black Rain*, not producing it, which I'd been doing on various levels as far back as *Blade Runner*. In a way, it was like a busman's holiday. I had a lot of fun on *Black Rain*."

As with the Tom Berenger character in *Someone To Watch Over Me, Black Rain* featured a central character, a cop, who was struggling to cope

54

with conflicts in his life and job. It was the kind of personal focus on characters which Scott's critics often claim his films lack. Michael Douglas played Nick Conklin, a New York cop who is taking bribes, justifying his actions by his ever-increasing lifestyle expenses, including payments to support his ex-wife and child, as well as housing and other costs. He's given the task of escorting a Japanese gangster, Sato, a member of the yakuza in American custody, back to police custody in Japan.

Accompanying the ethically compromised Conklin on the trip is the eager, clean young cop Charlie Vincent. After arriving at Osaka airport, Sato manages to escape from the pair, resulting in the American cops having to pursue their quarry through a disorienting foreign culture. Helping them in their search is Masahiro Matsumoto (Japanese action star Ken Takakura), a modest Japanese detective who both teaches and learns from the gaijin law enforcers visiting his country.

Development: Casting was the key to *Black Rain* as far as Ridley Scott was concerned. Signing up American stars Michael Douglas and Andy Garcia was the easy part. The director was aware that if he wanted the film to genuinely work, he'd have to be careful in filling the Japanese roles. Filming on location in Japan was also to be important to the film, but was also to be a source of frustration for the film-maker.

The first Japanese actor who came to Scott's mind was Ken Takakura, whom he knew from Sydney Pollock's 1975 film *The Yakuza*, as well as many 1970s Japanese yakuza (gangster) movies. However, over 200 Japanese actors auditioned for the role, even though many of them regarded the requirement to audition to be an 'insult'.

For the pivotal part of Sato, Scott turned to Yasuka Matsuda, an actor the director claimed was "essentially a comedian, known for a very amusing television series. He was a bit of an icon with the female population, very popular in Japan. Personally, he was a really nice guy." This "nice guy" was, however, pegged by Scott as the villain of the piece. Matsuda had also featured in several Japanese films since the mid-1970s, so he was well used to the demands of film roles.

His part in the film wasn't secure, despite the fact that Ridley Scott wanted the actor for the role. During June 1988, Yusaku Matsuda met with the American casting director, only to fail to win the part at this first audition. Matsuda then auditioned for Ridley Scott and producer Stanley Jaffe later in July. Scott recalled: "I knew intuitively, he was Sato, from the first moment I saw him, even before we talked. It was the same feeling I had when I first saw Rutger Hauer [for *Blade Runner*]."

The three final candidates for the role of Sato then auditioned with lead actor Michael Douglas. Scott had already decided on Matsuda, but he needed to win the agreement of Douglas and Jaffe. At the audition, Matsuda asked Douglas to lend him his necktie, explaining, "I'd like to use it instead of handcuffs. Actually, I would like to tie my hand with yours." Douglas was surprised, but impressed with Matsuda's improvisations. That night, Matsuda told his wife, "It was great! Michael Douglas was really wonderful! He was getting absorbed in his performance. I did my best playing with him, though much of what we did was ad lib. I feel, even if I lose the part, tonight was enough." While he was at a rehearsal for a TV drama, his producer and manager, Mitsuru Kurowasa, called to tell him he had won the part of Sato in *Black Rain*.

Shortly after being cast in the film, Matsuda was diagnosed with cancer, but decided to continue with the film, postponing his treatment. At a press conference to promote the movie, he said "I'm glad to appear in an international film. Movies are the common language of the world. I'm happy to be working with a director who understands my nuance." Yusaku Matsuda relished the role of Sato, bringing to life the film's over-the-top villain. He's a violent, yet comic-book creation, which wouldn't have been the same played by another actor. Unfortunately, it was one of Matsuda's final roles as he died in 1989 shortly after the release of *Black Rain* in the US.

As the Japanese crime boss who requires Conklin's subservience before he'll help in bringing Sato to justice, Scott cast Tomisaburo Wakayama, another Japanese celebrity known for the Lone Wolf (or 'baby cart') series of films in which a Samurai warrior travels Medieval Japan with his infant son in tow. Wakayama played Sugai and was himself an expert swordsman. It is Sugai who articulates the film's theme of cultural imperialism when he laments the harm done to Japan by America, from the dropping of the two atomic bombs which ended World War Two through decades of post-war cultural influence.

Securing the services of Wakayama for *Black Rain* (in the sympathetic role as the film's Virgil who guides Conklin and Vincent through Japan's criminal inferno) saw Scott participating in a ritual visit which sounds like a scene from the film itself. "Stars like [Wakayama] are kind of a law unto themselves in Japan," noted Scott. "He was very formal during our first meeting, which is when I asked him to be in *Black Rain*. It was a little weird, like a drama being acted out." Scott's audience with the chain-smoking actor took a while, with the actor acknowledging everything the director said with a barely perceptible nod of the head. "At the end, he said something to the translator in Japanese, which meant 'Yes, I'll do it.' And that was it."

Production: Shooting on the film started on location in Osaka in late October 1988, but the film's theme of clashing cultures seemed to be re-enacted in real life during the six weeks of shooting in Osaka and Kobe. The failure of communication between the American and Japanese members of the film crew led to the wrapping of shooting in Japan, early and abruptly, in early December 1988. "I think the main problem we had on *Black Rain* was with us, the American side of the production," admitted Scott much later. "We misunderstood the Japanese. I had an entirely Japanese crew, except for a few key people like Director of Photography [later director] Jan de Bont. There was also a misunderstanding of how costly it would be [to shoot] in Japan."

The solution to the cost overruns and breakdown in communication between the producers, director and crew was to relocate the production back in Los Angeles. Here, things could be more tightly controlled, with areas in Los Angeles, the Napa Valley and San Francisco doubling for the script's required remaining Japanese locations. It was a drastic solution, but one which worked for the film and doesn't become apparent in the finished movie. Filming finally wrapped in mid-March 1989 in San Francisco.

On the last weekend of shooting, Michael Douglas invited 18 members of the cast to a restaurant for a celebratory meal. The only Japanese there were Yusaku Matsuda and Ken Takakura, as they were the only Japanese actors who attended shooting from the beginning (at Osaka) to the end (at Napa). Michael Douglas made T-shirts as a surprise present for everyone. The black shirts were printed 'Survivors of *Black Rain*', and the back itemised the shooting locations: Osaka, Kobe, New York, Hollywood, Napa and San Francisco.

Reshoots: The climax of *Black Rain* was reshot, at the suggestion of the Paramount executives who'd given the film the green light in the first place. Sherry Lansing and Sydney Jaffe were discomfited by the violent dénouement which Ridley Scott presented in the first cut of the film. In the rain drenched battle between Conklin and Sato, the American policeman actually impaled the Japanese gangster on a fence post. The Paramount executives felt this scene meant that the film lacked a satisfying conclusion, as the villain escaped justice and the American 'hero' remained a flawed, immoral character at the film's end. Instead, extra scenes were shot, revealing that Douglas' character instead spares Sato and even allows his Japanese colleague Matsumoto to turn the gangster into the authorities.

"Douglas killing Sato didn't really jibe very well with the idea that Michael's character becomes a better person during his trip to Japan," admitted Scott, agreeing with the interference of a producer for the first time on one of his films. "I cut out Sato's death scene and shot additional footage, showing Douglas and Ken delivering Sato to the Osaka police."

The loss of this controversial scene certainly robbed *Black Rain* of its violent climax, but the film remained one of Scott's most violent pictures, at least until he made *Gladiator*. Sato's penchant for knives meant that the film was packed with many little and a few large violent moments. "Everyone knew that *Black Rain* was going to be a bit more violent than most of my films going in," claimed Scott. "That was strictly a reflection of the script. "

Reception: *Black Rain* was released in America in September 1989, to mixed critical notices. Roger Ebert, of *The Chicago Sun-Times*, trotted out a familiar criticism: 'The production design is so overwhelming that the characters seem lost and upstaged; frequently the humans are not even the most interesting things on the screen. I would probably have enjoyed the visuals if they served any purpose (I admired the look of *Blade Runner*), but they're just show-off virtuosity.' Ebert, normally a fan of Ridley Scott's work, didn't even like the lead character of *Black Rain*, 'This is a designer movie, all look and no heart, and the Douglas character is curiously unsympathetic.'

With its Japanese influences, cops and wet cityscapes, certain audiences couldn't help but look at *Black Rain* as a contemporary remake of *Blade Runner* in thriller guise. The film even shared the same initials in the title. Rita Kempley of *The Washington Post* noticed the similarities: '*Black Rain* is chock-full of moments, jazzy scenery and snazzy bits of dialogue, and stuffed with steroids. It's big, maybe too big for its shallow notions and commonplace structure. But it is also beautiful and terrible in the same ways that other Scott movies have been eye-filling. With its teeming Asian landscape, its dark kaleidoscopic palette and its heavily layered composition, it's reminiscent of *Blade Runner*.' *Entertainment Weekly* agreed with this assessment: 'Scott paints gorgeous pictures with light – *Black Rain* resembles Scott's *Blade Runner* without the sci-fi film noir atmosphere, that is, without the imagination.'

Despite the negative critical reaction, *Black Rain* was to prove to be a hit with US audiences. The culture clash elements also brought depth to a film lacking from most thrillers, and certainly missing from *Someone To Watch Over Me*. As a result, the film took $45 million at the box office in the US, marking something of a recovery in Ridley Scott's commercial fortunes.

Thelma & Louise (1991)

"Every time we get in trouble, you go blank or plead insanity."

– Louise to Thelma, *Thelma & Louise*.

Director: Ridley Scott, Writer: Callie Khouri

Cast: Susan Sarandon (Louise Sawyer), Geena Davis (Thelma Dickinson), Harvey Keitel (Hal Slocumb), Michael Madsen (Jimmy), Christopher McDonald (Darryl), Stephen Tobolowsky (Max), Brad Pitt (J D), Timothy Carhart (Harlan Puckett), Lucinda Jenney (Lena, the Waitress), Jason Beghe (State Trooper)

Crew: Producers: Callie Khouri (Co-Producer), Dean O'Brien (Co-Producer), Mimi Polk, Ridley Scott; Music: Hans Zimmer; Cinematography: Adrian Biddle; Editing: Thom Noble; Production Design: Norris Spencer; Art Direction: Lisa Dean; Costume Design: Elizabeth McBride

Plot: Gender-switch road movie which sees two women on the run from the cops seeking their destiny across America.

Inspiration: As always, Ridley Scott had a strong reason for the selection of his next project – and it was a reason he was able to apply to almost every film he directed. "The main reason I chose to do this film [*Thelma & Louise*]," said Scott, "was that I'd never done anything like it before. This is a film where the emphasis – the driving force, if you will – is almost totally on character, rather than where a spaceship comes from."

Thelma & Louise was to prove to be a feminist spin on that most masculine of film genres, the road movie. The script, a tale of two gun-toting women on the run, attracted Scott's attention as soon as he started reading it. "Rarely do scripts come along that are about truth," noted Scott. "This one most certainly is and it never deviates from that. It's humorous, it's dramatic, it's even slightly mythical in proportions. That's just about everything you can ask for from a really good story."

This story came from the pen of Callie Khouri, a then 33 year old with a background in music video production. She created the tale based on her own speculations as to how a single event could impact on a pair of women, causing them to choose between the lives they had and the lives they wanted. Central to Khouri's drama was Thelma Dickson a suburban housewife married to Darryl, a male chauvinist pig. However, Thelma isn't the contented housewife that husband Darryl thinks she is. Her best friend, Louise Sawyer, provides the spark which changes Thelma's life. Louise is a coffee-shop waitress waiting for her life to begin and for her commitment-phobic boyfriend Jimmy to decide to settle down. Tired of waiting, she picks up Thelma for a wild weekend away from their menfolk. What neither anticipated is just how far their trip would take them.

Ridley Scott chose *Thelma & Louise* not only because it was unlike his previous films, but because it crystallised elements he'd dealt with before and brought them to light in a way he hadn't in his previous films. His films had always featured significant female characters such as Pris in *Blade Runner* and, of course, Ripley in *Alien*. The aspect of *Thelma & Louise* which Scott had not tackled before was the comedy. Although the pair go on the run after an attempted rape and manslaughter, the film is wickedly humorous in its skewering of male stereotypes. "It basically took apart the whole male species," admitted Scott.

It was a year after the release of *Black Rain* before Scott turned his attention to making *Thelma & Louise*. He'd taken time out from feature film-making to further develop his advertising production house, RSA, which had opened an LA office towards the end of the 1980s. It was producer Mimi Polk, who worked on *Someone To Watch Over Me* (and later *1492: Conquest Of Paradise* and *White Squall*), who brought the *Thelma & Louise* script to Scott's attention. "I'd been searching for a character-oriented script having very much to do with people," said Scott, showing a distinct awareness of his critical reputation as a director who paid much more attention to his visuals then to his characters or stories. "Each of the eight guys in *Thelma & Louise* actually represented a different portion of one whole man. I never felt that *Thelma & Louise* was anti-male or into male-bashing, although I do actually believe it was one of those screenplays that honestly dealt with what a lot of women have to put up with."

Casting: When casting the central roles Scott started considering some big name female stars, before deciding that they weren't suitable for the film. "I wanted the film to have a pseudo-documentary reality," claimed Scott of his ambitions for *Thelma & Louise*. "I felt audiences might have had trouble accepting super high-profile actresses in reality-based roles."

That meant looking for actors who could carry off the roles, but were perhaps less well known by moviegoers. One of the lead cast members actually came to Scott. "At the time," said Scott, "Geena Davis wasn't that big a star." That was in spite of her attention-grabbing turn in David Cronenberg's remake of *The Fly* (opposite then husband Jeff Goldblum) and her 1988 Best Supporting Actor Oscar for *The Accidental Tourist* (opposite William Hurt). "She has a genuine comedic gift, one of those actors who changes with the role. When Geena heard I was going to direct *Thelma & Louise*, she came in and saw me. Geena basically pitched us for the part, so I picked her first."

That left the task of finding a complimentary and experienced actress for the pivotal role of Louise, but one who wouldn't bring a lot of 'big star' baggage to the film. "Susan Sarandon is one of the best actresses we've got. She was the best pairing with Geena, and they got on like gangbusters. They genuinely enjoyed working with each other. I think you can see that in the film."

For the part of the sympathetic cop on the trail of the runaway women, Scott turned to *The Duellists* actor, Harvey Keitel. Geena Davis recommended actor Christopher MacDonald for the perhaps thankless role of Darryl (the actors had previously had a relationship), and Scott was happy to go with her suggestion. For Jimmy, Louise's reluctant boyfriend, Scott cast Michael Madsen for his smouldering good looks and emotional reserve.

Production: Principal photography on *Thelma & Louise* began on Monday 11 June 1990 in Tarzana, California, a residential suburb which doubled in the film as Thelma's small-town Arkansas neighbourhood. For six weeks the production took over the town, using homes, businesses and public buildings throughout the Southern California area, including the Silver Bullet Saloon in Long Beach and the famous DuPar's restaurant in Thousand Oaks, which featured in the film as the coffee shop where Louise worked. A switch of location took the production unit to Bakersfield, where a variety of locations from the local oil fields to the lush greenery of the San Joaquin Valley, served as the roadside stops featured throughout the film.

"During pre-production of the film, we travelled the exact route taken by the characters in the film," said Scott, revealing his exacting attention to detail. Aware it was impractical to actually make the film along the real route, Scott was determined that he would capture the look and feel of places along the way in the film.

By August, the crew of around 175 people had relocated to Moad in Utah, a former uranium mining town situated on the banks of the Colorado River. The town doubled for sites in the film which were supposed to be in Arizona and New Mexico. "Southern California and south eastern Utah each provided innumerable locations stemming from one particular base. Although we did shoot at many different sites, logistically speaking it would have been much more difficult to move from state to state."

One actor emerged from the film a fully blown star: Brad Pitt. Cast by Ridley Scott as suave highwayman J D in preference to original choice Daniel Baldwin, Pitt sweeps Davis' Thelma off her feet and then relieves her of her $6,000 savings. Brad Pitt was not particularly well known prior to

Thelma & Louise, but the scene in which J D seduces the older but more innocent Thelma, made him a household name. "Ridley would let us play around a lot," said Pitt of his director, who spent a lot of time on what he knew was a scene pivotal to the story. "He'd say, 'OK, we got that one. Let's try something else.' I'm having trouble living up to that '$6,000 orgasm'. I prefer to look at the film as about people in dead-end situations, and then an event puts them on a different path. They can become victims of that or they can take control of it."

Location shooting of the film wrapped 12 weeks later on 31 August 1990, and with a low budget of just $16 million to content with, *Thelma & Louise* had been a relatively quick shoot.

"*Thelma & Louise* was the best time I had working on a movie since my first film," admitted Scott, happy to have finally found a film that was both commercially and critically successful on first release. "I thoroughly enjoyed myself. I think everybody else had a wonderful time too. And it went like lightning."

That Ending! The ending of *Thelma & Louise* was to prove controversial, not only with audiences but with Ridley Scott himself. As the car the pair of outlaws are driving, a 1966 Thunderbird, reaches the end of the road pursued by the police, the fugitives decide to keep going. The film ends on a triumphal note, freeze-framing on the car, caught in mid-air before it falls into the ravine.

That wasn't the original ending, though. As with *Black Rain* and *Blade Runner* before it, Scott had a tougher ending in mind originally. As he shot it, the action continued beyond the now famous freeze-frame image, following the Thunderbird as it crashes into the canyon and cutting to reaction shots of Harvey Keitel, dismayed at the deaths of the runaways.

That version of the film ended with a return to the opening shot of the movie: the empty road stretching into the distance. "I put in that shot at the beginning of *Thelma & Louise* as sort of a visual metaphor," said Scott. "It suggested the freedom these women were after."

Scott rethought this ending, though. "I realised it undercut the emotion of Thelma and Louise's final gesture somehow," admitted Scott. "That additional footage diminished the nobility of their decision to stay free and drive over the edge. I cut the conclusion back a bit, ending on the freeze-frame of their car taking off into space. When we previewed the film, we got a lot of cards [preview audience comment cards] saying 'Whatever you do, don't change the ending. It's the antithesis of a Hollywood ending, it's the right ending.'"

Reception: *Thelma & Louise* was easily one of the most controversial films made by Ridley Scott. The women versus men opposition of the film generated acres of newspaper and magazine coverage, giving the film a huge amount of free publicity. According to *Entertainment Weekly*: '*Thelma & Louise* wants to be the female-buddy movie to end all female-buddy movies. And maybe it is. At once extravagant and shallow, hilarious and glib, mythical and weirdly synthetic, this flamboyant saga of outlaw heroines on the run exerts a cracked fascination.'

For once, Ridley Scott found himself being praised for the characters in his film over the visual splendour. 'Scott keeps this lost weekend from hell varied, rich and character-driven,' wrote Deeson Howe in *The Washington Post*. '*Thelma & Louise* may look like just another girl-buddy road picture, but in director Ridley Scott's hands, it's propulsively more with stirring undertones about oppressed women. Humour is mixed adroitly with existential ominousness; every character is lively. *Thelma & Louise* is unabashed, streamlined entertainment.' Reviews like that brought in over $45 million at the US box office, matching the success of *Black Rain*.

The controversy around the film was another reason Scott singled out *Thelma & Louise* as one of his favourites among his own films. "When I think of *Thelma & Louise* now, I realise we really touched a nerve with that picture," said Scott. "I was happiest that we'd made a funny film. The politics were really secondary to that. I just enjoyed the hell out of making a comedy, and discovering that I could make it look good at the same time."

5. The Pathfinders Trilogy

1492: Conquest Of Paradise (1992)

"Asia can be found to the west"

– Christopher Columbus, *1492: Conquest Of Paradise.*

Director: Ridley Scott, Writer: Roselyne Bosch

Cast: Gérard Depardieu (Columbus), Armand Assante (Sanchez), Sigourney Weaver (Queen Isabel), Loren Dean (Older Fernando), Angela Molina (Beatrix), Fernando Rey (Marchena), Michael Wincott (Noxica), Tchéky Karyo (Pinzon), Kevin Dunn (Capt. Mendez), Frank Langella (Santangel), Mark Margolis (Bobadilla), Kario Salem (Arojaz), Billy L Sullivan (Fernando, aged 10), John Heffernan (Brother Buyl), Arnold Vosloo (Guevara), Steven Waddington (Bartolome), Fernando Guillén Cuervo (Giacomo), José Luis Ferrer (Alonso), Bercelio Moya (Utapan), Juan Diego Botto (Diego), Achero Mañas (Ships Boy), Fernando García Rimada (King Ferdinand), Albert Vidal (Hernando de Talavera), Isabel Prinz (Duenna), Ángela Rosal (Pinzon's Wife), Jack Taylor (Vicuna)

Crew: Producers: Roselyne Bosch (Co-Producer), Marc Boyman (Co-Producer), Pere Fages (Co-Producer), Alain Goldman, Mimi Polk Scotela (Executive), Ridley Scott, Iain Smith (Executive), Garth Thomas (Associate); Original Music: Vangelis; Cinematography: Adrian Biddle; Film Editing: William M Anderson, Françoise Bonnot; Production Design: Norris Spencer; Art Direction: Martin Hitchcock, Raúl Antonio Paton, Kevin Phipps, Luke Scott; Costume Design: Charles Knode, Barbara Rutter

Plot: In 1492, Columbus sails the ocean blue. Seeking the Orient, 15th Century explorer Christopher Columbus discovers the New World instead and is given a hero's welcome by Queen Isabel and King Ferdinand upon his return. That's the popular version of the story, but the film of *1492* covers Columbus' struggles to finance his voyage, the machinations of those who supported and opposed him and the setbacks and decline of his later years, which saw him forgotten, having sunk into obscurity.

Inspiration: It may be accurate historically and wear its impressive research on its sleeve, and it may boast Ridley Scott's trademark stunning visuals and atmospheres, but for many, *1492: The Conquest Of Paradise* was the beginning of an artistic and commercial decline for the director, which was only halted with the blockbuster *Gladiator*.

Roselyne Bosch, a French journalist, had travelled to Spain in 1987 for the weekly news magazine *Le Point* to cover the 500th anniversary of the maiden voyage of Christopher Columbus. Although he lived in Spain, the 15th Century navigator was Italian-born and best known by the public for his discovery of America. The more complex political story of the journey of Columbus was not as widely known, and it was this which came to intrigue Bosch as it would Ridley Scott.

Drawing on previously unrevealed archive material, including letters in Columbus' own handwriting, Bosch decided to write a screenplay charting the two voyages Columbus made to the Americas, but focusing as much on the politics of his adopted homeland as on his discovery of the New World. As a central character, Bosch also discovered in Columbus a deeply conflicted man who was both an explorer and in favour of the savage colonisation of his discovered lands. In Bosch's hands, Columbus was to be a character brought to grief by his own hand.

Bosch tried, in the late 1980s, to interest French film producers in the project, but none were taken by the enterprise. Finally, by the start of the new decade, Alain Goldman had brought the script to the attention of Ridley Scott.

For his part, Scott was already considering developing a project on Columbus, aware that 1992 would be the 500th anniversary of the voyage, so he was delighted when a ready-formed script dropped onto his lap. For Scott, this project would be a return to the historical milieu of his first feature film, *The Duellists*, and an escape from the glossy contemporary cop thriller genre which he was afraid he was in danger of becoming trapped in, even with the success of *Thelma & Louise*.

Production: The key to the film, in many respects, would be the casting of the central role: who could play a larger-then-life character like Columbus. Only one actor occurred to Scott: Frenchman Gérard Depardieu. "I couldn't think of anyone else being that big, in terms of having the proper energy and outsized personality for the Columbus character," noted Scott. "Gérard Depardieu is Columbus. He is an extremely passionate character driven almost purely by his intuition."

Despite the director being British and the star French, *1492* was an American movie. The casting of a Frenchman in the lead, therefore, meant a strong line-up of American actors was required. Chief among them was Sigourney Weaver, returning from Scott's *Alien* for the role of Queen Isabel of Spain (she won the role after Scott's first choice, Angelica Huston, wavered about taking the part). Important supporting roles went to Armand Assante as Sanchez, who introduced Columbus to the Queen of Spain and Michael Wincott as Noxica, whose name served to sum up his character.

For the first time, Scott went down the independent financing route for *1492*. The money to make the film was raised by pre-selling international distribution rights at the 1991 Cannes Film Festival, to supplement the $10 million paid by Paramount for the American rights and the $11 million raised through French company Gaumont who bought the French distribution rights.

Although interiors were shot at Pinewood Studios just outside London, locations were extremely important to the look of *1492*. Spain, the Dominican republic and Costa Rica all stood in for various locales in the 'New World.' December 1991 saw the beginning of filming in a 16th century Spanish villa in the town of Cáceres, doubling for a monastery. Eighty-two days later, the film wrapped.

There was a surprise for Ridley Scott in the form of not one, but two competing Columbus-based films. One was just as serious, if duller, than *1492*, while the other saw the attempted resurrection of the *Carry On...* series of British 'saucy' humour films. Both *Christopher Columbus: The Discovery* and *Carry On Columbus* flopped upon release, but the mere fact of competing films, with all three attempting to capitalise on the 500th anniversary, was an irritation to Scott. "I tried to ignore the other films and just got on with it," said Scott. "I actually enjoyed [making *1492*]. How often does one get to find a working replica of the Nina." Scott found the replica in Brazil where it had been recreated by a Christopher Columbus Society. The other two ships, the Pinta and the Santa Maria, had to be built especially for the production.

The biggest challenge for the director and crew of *1492* was recreating the America which Columbus found. The Costa Rican coast stood in for the first colony Columbus established on Hispanola (Haiti and the Dominican Republic today). The re-creation of the world before and after Columbus' arrival was one of the most satisfying elements of *1492*.

Another was the musical score which stands up strongly as an entity separate from the film in its own right. For the score, Scott turned to Vangelis, whom he had worked very successfully with on *Blade Runner*. "Working with directors is a question of compatibility," noted the composer. "You need to have a positive exchange of ideas to achieve the correct result. One thing that I would like to see happen with films is for music not to be treated as just one more ingredient, but as an integral and fundamental part, due to its fatal capacity to affect the mood of the movie."

Having provided the soundtrack for the future, Scott believed that Vangelis was the right composer to score his vision of the past. "This film could have had a traditional score to suit its 15th Century subject," admitted Scott. "That's the last thing I wanted. I knew Vangelis could give me something which was both appropriate for the period and is also contemporary. I hate it when people say you shouldn't notice the score. The score, if it's doing its job, should lift and elevate the movie."

Reception: Released on 2 October 1992, just a week before the 500th anniversary of the original voyage, *1492: Conquest Of Paradise* was met with a very muted response. The mix of complex political intrigue, a French actor in the lead (*Green Card*, also starring Depardieu had been a less than stellar hit in America) and a lack of the derring-do adventure which audiences might have expected contributed to the film's commercial failure. The confusion caused by the competing Columbus films can't have helped the situation, either.

In its review, *The Washington Post* called *1492* 'sumptuous but vacuous' and went on to comment: 'Though Columbus was the dreamer and pioneer who first set foot in the New World and brought treasures and territory to Spain, he died all but forgotten. The movie, alas, for all its wondrous beauty, is destined to suffer a similar fate.' Roger Ebert of *The Chicago-Sun Times* had more positive things to say about *1492* than most critics: 'Ridley Scott's *1492: Conquest Of Paradise* sees Christopher Columbus as more complex and humane than in the other screen treatments of the character. What disappoints me a little about Scott's version is that he seems to hurry past Columbus' actual voyage of discovery. Ridley Scott is a visually oriented director who finds great beauty in his vision of the New World, including a breathtaking shot in which the ocean mists rise to reveal a verdant shore. In its own way and up to a certain point, *1492* is a satisfactory film. Depardieu lends it gravity, the supporting performances are convincing, the locations are realistic, and we are inspired to reflect that it did indeed take a certain nerve to sail off into nowhere.'

Facts And Figures:

• A paltry $7 million box-office take was all that *1492* could manage on its blink-and-you'll-miss-it cinema release, against a below-the-line (production excluding prints and advertising) cost of $44 million. Overall, the film took only $52 million worldwide, a disappointing result.

• The fact that Ridley Scott had once again confounded his audience's expectations by producing a surprising and altogether different film to his last is perhaps the strongest lesson to be drawn from *1492*. Although a historical epic, this wasn't *The Duellists* and it certainly wasn't *Alien* or *Thelma & Louise*. Instead, *1492: The Conquest Of Paradise* is what Ridley Scott set out to make: a unique account of a pivotal moment in world history.

White Squall (1996)

"How many boys did you lose...? And how come you didn't go down with your ship?"

– Reporter, *White Squall*.

Director: Ridley Scott, Writer: Chuck Gieg (Memoirs), Todd Robinson

Cast: Jeff Bridges (Captain Christopher 'Skipper' Sheldon), Caroline Goodall (Dr. Alice Sheldon), John Savage (McCrea), Scott Wolf (Chuck Gieg), Jeremy Sisto (Frank Beaumont), Ryan Phillippe (Gil Martin), David Lascher (Robert March), Eric Michael Cole (Dean Preston), Jason Marsden (Shay Jennings), David Selby (Francis Beaumont), Julio Oscar Mechoso (Girard Pascal), Zeljko Ivanek (Sanders), Balthazar Getty (Tod Johnstone), Ethan Embry (Tracy Lapchick), Jordan Clarke (Charles Gieg), Lizbeth MacKay (Middy Gieg), Jill Larson (Peggy Beaumont), James Medina (Cuban Commander), James Rebhorn (Tyler), Nicole Ann Samuel (Girl In Brothel), Becky Ann Baker (Ms. Boyde), Camilla Overbye Roos (Bregitta)

Crew: Producers: Mimi Polk Gitlin, Rocky Lang, Terry Needham (Associate), Todd Robinson (Co-Producer), Ridley Scott (Executive), Nigel Wooll (Co-Producer); Original Music: Jeff Rona; Cinematography: Hugh Johnson; Film Editing: Gerry Hambling; Production Design: Peter J Hampton, Leslie Tomkins; Costume Design: Judianna Makovsky

Plot: A group of troubled young men sail halfway around the world on a windjammer one summer in 1960. During their spectacular odyssey they learn life lessons from a stern captain, their teachers aboard ship, and nature herself when they encounter a freak storm known as a 'white squall.' Based on a true story.

Inspiration: A multi-film deal between Ridley Scott, his brother Tony (by now a film-maker in his own right with *The Hunger* and *Top Gun* among other films under his belt) and 20th Century Fox led the director to begin developing a series of new potential film projects.

Scott's attention had been caught by an October 1992 *New Yorker* article by Richard Preston entitled *Crisis In The Hot Zone*. The feature, which Preston later expanded into a 1994 best-selling book, dealt with the true story of an outbreak of the Ebola virus, a deadly disease which could kill those infected within days. The story told how scientists at the US Veterinary Corp in Virginia (not too far from the US seat of power in Washington, DC) discovered their test monkeys carried a strain of the virus which threatened to get out of control and contaminate, or even escape, the labs.

Scott leapt on the project, sensing that it had the making of a very good science-based thriller with the added advantage of being based on real events. The rights to the article were purchased and Scott assembled a team to make the film, with Lynda Obst producing, *Dracula* writer James V Hart writing the screenplay and actress Jodie Foster signed up to star. The virus project was to be short-lived however, as rival producer Arnold Kopelson launched his own fictional version of the Ebola scare, entitled *Outbreak*. Kopelson had been after the film rights to the Preston article, but Scott beat him to the punch. Not wanting the facts to get in the way of a good film, Kopelson set out to outdo real life by inventing a similar scenario. Wolfgang Peterson directed the film, Dustin Hoffman starred and *Outbreak* proved to be the nail in the coffin of Scott's *Hot Zone* project. Having just experienced the problems that a rival film on the same subject could cause with *1492: Conquest Of Paradise*, Scott was not prepared to fight that kind of battle again.

As it was Scott's film was running into trouble anyway. He'd managed to attract Robert Redford as the male lead to co-star alongside Foster, only for the pair to clash over the script, with Redford threatening to bring his own team of screenwriters onto the project. With the conflict growing and the rival film already entering production, Scott threw in the towel, giving 20th Century Fox the ideal excuse to terminate the *Hot Zone* project.

While keeping an eye out for other features to direct, Scott turned to producing, turning out two films on which he served as Executive Producer. The first was *Monkey Trouble*, a little-seen 1994 film about the adventures of a young girl and her mischievous pet monkey. The second was a remake of the 1951 drama *The Browning Version*, directed by Mike Figgis and starring Albert Finney.

If to Scott's fans and supporters this activity seemed like so much treading water, what was to come next would be something of a surprise. Far from directing a new film and returning to his glory days of *Alien, Blade Runner* and even *Legend* as his fans wanted, Ridley Scott decided to buy his own film studio. He and brother Tony headed up a consortium which, in 1995, purchased Shepperton Studios in London. "I'd been coming to Shepperton for 25 years," said Scott, "I was one of their best customers. I had a soft spot in my heart for it, as it was where I shot my first real studio movie (*Alien*). We've since done a lot of upgrading to the place."

The studio purchase was an investment and a safety net. It gave Scott an income, by renting the facility to other film-makers, which would prove useful and it gave him access to state-of-the-art facilities should he ever need them for any of his future projects. Shepperton was to prove to be an asset for Ridley Scott Associates, the like of which he could only have dreamt of owning when he first set out on his film-making career. Only half-joking, Scott called his purchase of Shepperton "Payback time. Hollywood is only a bloody village, yet it has a massive movie business. I thought, 'Why haven't we got a billion dollar film industry in the UK?' The US used to account for 75 per cent of a film's market. Now that balance is evening out. I want to bring pride back to the British industry." With his business head on, Scott saw buying the studio complex as a shrewd investment. "There's such a film culture in London that the American studios are beginning to realise that they get a better bang for their dollar in the UK," claimed Scott, while maintaining a realistic approach. "I'm not a fool. It's not sheer patriotism. It's the right time for me to get involved."

Scott did find a new project to develop in late 1994, just before finalising the deal on Shepperton. *White Squall* was an original screenplay sent to the director by first-time screenwriter Todd Robinson. Like the abandoned *Hot Zone* project, *White Squall* was based on true events. In this case, a 1960 boat trip which resulted in the death of six members of the crew: pupils and teachers from one of America's top 'prep' schools. After the storm in which the Albatross was caught, the Captain faced a new storm back on shore when he was tried (and eventually acquitted) of criminal negligence.

Having been upset at the demise of his *Hot Zone* project, Ridley Scott was perhaps a bit too quick in jumping to agree to make the next attractive 'true story' film that came along. "I'd become anxious to prove that our production company could kick in another movie fairly quickly," admitted Scott of the commercial pressures which he felt were acting upon his decision-making process. "I looked around and found two pieces of material. One was called *Mulholland Falls* (a period thriller directed in 1996 by Lee Tamahori) and the other was *White Squall*. I choose *Squall* because the more I thought about it, the more I realised Robinson's script showed the Albatross boys making a difficult transition into manhood in a very unusual way. Their rites-of-passage story had been approached very earnestly... without being sentimental. I responded very well to that."

Following Tom Berenger and Gérard Depardieu, Scott chose another less than stellar leading man for his film. "I think Jeff Bridges is one of the best actors in America," claimed Scott in defence of his choice to play the put-upon Captain Sheldon. "What's really remarkable about him is that Jeff always finds a unique character in each piece he does." While Scott may be right about Bridges' acting abilities, he wasn't exactly the kind of star who could open a film. He's no Mel Gibson, Kevin Costner or Harrison Ford. While he has his fans and key films like *The Fabulous Baker Boys, Tucker: The Man And His Dream, Starman* and the innovative computer-animated Disney movie *Tron*, Jeff Bridges was not a strong enough lead to carry off *White Squall*, especially when the rest of the cast was to be made up of unknown teens in the days before the outbreak of teen-orientated cinema which has plagued the late 1990s and into the new century.

The teens in the film were played by Scott Wolf, Ryan Phillippe, Jeremy Sisto and Balthazar Getty – all actors who would later go on to greater fame (or in some cases, like Getty, infamy), but who at the time were relatively unknown except through the occasional TV series. It was a big risk for Scott to stake his $36 million adventure film on the unproven talents of a group of teens.

Production: The production of *White Squall* was never going to be easy: films which require lots of water or are set on or around boats are notoriously difficult (*Jaws, Waterworld, The Abyss* and *Titanic* all spring to mind as difficult productions which share that one element). Principal photography took place in mid-1995, with locations around the coast of America, including Georgia, South Carolina and the Bahamas being used to recreate the fateful journey of the Albatross. Most of the filming, however, took place in the West Indies, particularly around the Caribbean islands of St Lucia, St Vincent and Grenada. Filming even extended to the Cape of Good Hope in Africa to capture shots of the Albatross encountering 40-foot waves and heavy seas.

The boat used had seen service in several previous films, including *The Blue Lagoon* and *Taipan*. The New Zealand-owned boat was called the Eye of the Wind and it proved to be a fortuitous find for Ridley Scott. "The most difficult thing about doing *White Squall* was finding locations that hadn't been ruined by cruise lines," lamented Scott. "Where you find cruise ships, that's the beginning of the end – beautiful areas that used to have untouched towns and harbours are now filled with condos and posh Yves St Laurent shops."

Tempted to push his film-making skills to the limits by filming the climax of the action in the midst of a real storm, Scott decided to settle for recreating the adverse climatic conditions he required in the Mediterranean Studios in Malta, often used by Hollywood studios for complex water work. He'd return to Malta to film much of *Gladiator*.

"According to the real Captain Sheldon (who was an advisor on the film), the real squall had been like a gigantic down draught," recalled Scott. "It just sprang out of nowhere, hit the water and created a strange, flatten-

71

ing effect, like the opposite of a tidal wave. Then it hit the Albatross and the wind took the ship right over." Four weeks of the 14-week shoot were spent on this complex sequence in the Malta studios which had previously been used for *Clash Of The Titans* and Robert Altman's *Popeye*. The use of a full-size replica mounted on a series of complex gimbals in the water tank and cleverly filmed miniatures served to bring the disaster to life. Other effects featured in the film included an animatronic dolphin and digital effects by Peerless Optical, e.g. dramatic rain and lightning effects.

Reception: Unfortunately, when the film opened at the American box office, it seemed as if its potential audience had also taken a holiday. The film, released in the US on 2 February 1996, flopped, taking a poor $10 million. By the end of its release, *White Squall* had grossed only $40 million worldwide, a very poor showing for such a dramatic and high-profile film from such a talented director.

Contributing to the low impact of the film were the damning reviews. *USA Today* saw the film as one of Scott's lesser works: 'Sporadically great film-maker Ridley Scott spits in the face of any potential water phobia with the middling *White Squall*,' said the newspaper. 'Fortunately, the 15-minute squall is spectacular and the movie's partial redeemer.' *Time* couldn't work out why Ridley Scott had made the film: '*White Squall* is based on a true story, but invested as it is with relentlessly clichéd emotions, it plays like cheap fiction. What a sometime visionary like Scott is doing mixed up with it is hard to fathom.' *The Washington Post* agreed: 'It's disappointing that a director with the vision of Ridley *Blade Runner* Scott and an actor with the depth of Jeff Bridges conspired to produce such a sodden venture.' *The Chicago-Sun Times* critic Roger Ebert did have good things to say about *White Squall*: 'I enjoyed the movie for the sheer physical exuberance of its adventure. It is magnificently mounted and photographed.'

G. I. Jane (1997)

"The best thing about pain, it tells you you're not dead yet."

– Master Chief John Urgayle, *G. I. Jane*.

Director: Ridley Scott, Writers: Danielle Alexandra (Story), David Twohy & Danielle Alexandra (Screenplay)

Cast: Demi Moore (Lieutenant Jordan O'Neil), Viggo Mortensen (Master Chief John Urgayle), Anne Bancroft (Senator Lillian DeHaven), Jason Beghe (Royce), Daniel von Bargen (Theodore Hayes), John Michael Higgins (Chief Of Staff), Kevin Gage (Instructor Pyro), David Warshofsky (Instructor Johns), David Vadim (Cortez), Morris Chestnut (McCool), Josh Hopkins (Flea), James Caviezel (Slovnik), Boyd Kestner (Wickwire), Angel David (Newberry), Stephen Ramsey (Stamm), Gregg Bello (Miller), Scott Wilson (CO Salem), Lucinda Jenney (Blondell)

Crew: Producers: Danielle Alexandra (Executive), Julie Bergman Sender (Executive), Roger Birnbaum, Diane Minter Lewis (Associate), Tim McBride (Associate), Demi Moore, Terry Needham (Associate), Ridley Scott, Suzanne Todd, Nigel Wooll (Co-Producer), Chris Zarpas (Executive); Original Music: Trevor Jones; Music: Giacomo Puccini (from opera 'Gianni Schicchi'); Cinematography: Hugh Johnson; Film Editing: Pietro Scalia; Production Design: Arthur Max; Art Direction: Richard Johnson; Costume Design: Marilyn Vance

Plot: Navy Lieutenant Jordan O'Neil is the first female candidate for SEAL training, but her biggest battles are yet to come: brutal training regimens, persecution from her tough-as-nails Master Chief, and the growing realisation that she is a pawn in the political games played by her chief supporter, a hardened female Senator.

Inspiration: *G. I. Jane*, was drawn from contemporary newspaper headlines. Written by screenwriter Danielle Alexandra, the story drew from current political issues and news headlines about women serving in the American military in a combat role. "From day one, long before I sold the project and wrote the screenplay, there was never any question in my mind that anyone other than Demi Moore would play the role of Lt. Jordan O'Neil," claimed Alexandra. Luckily, Scott agreed as Alexandra had already approached the actress, then at the height of her fame and commercial success, to star in the movie. "I believed she was the only actress credible enough and capable of handling the physical and emotional ride," the writer continued.

For her part, Moore was ready to play a more demanding role, especially one which would draw on her physical strengths as well as her acting abilities. "I wasn't interested in just stepping into a man's character in an action movie. What *G. I. Jane* afforded me was the opportunity to deal not only with the enormous physical demands of the action genre, but also to be involved with something that had great substance. The story deals with a subject matter that is not only topical, but also very important because of the bigger issue of women having more choices available to them."

Danielle Alexandra saw her script become the centre of a frantic bidding war between rival studios. The subject matter was in the news and any film capitalising on a contemporary topic had to be made quickly in order to make a maximum impact. The winner of the process was Caravan Pictures, run by ex-studio head Joe Roth. Producer Roger Birnbaum took control of the project.

After several screenplay drafts by Alexandra, David Twohy made his creative contributions by enhancing the action elements of the story. Alexandra noted: "*G. I. Jane* was written by a woman, for a woman, about a woman; but what makes the screenplay so great is that you have David as the action writer, and me as the dramatic action, character writer. I genuinely believe that *G. I. Jane* is more special because it has this combination of writing in it. When you combine the two, you have a combustible piece of material."

Production: Having been more used to developing his own projects, Ridley Scott found himself a director for hire on *G. I. Jane*. Although presented with something of a fait accompli in the casting of Demi Moore, Ridley Scott had a free hand in casting the other roles the film required. For the part of Senator Lillian DeHaven, who recommends Lt. Jordan for Navy SEAL training expecting her to fail, Scott chose legendary actress Anne Bancroft. Bancroft was aware of Scott's work and saw in *G. I. Jane* some echoes of the director's work on *Thelma & Louise*. "I'm attracted to a role if I'm ready for it," she explained. "I recently had been playing a lot of women who stay at home, a mother, a great aunt, a grandmother. Here was a glamorous woman with a great sense of herself who is out in the world. It was nice to pull that out of myself."

The male lead in the film, Master Chief John Urgayle, fell to Viggo Mortensen, then relatively unknown. Scott said, "I'd had my eye on Viggo Mortensen since seeing him in *The Indian Runner*. It was a very dark movie, but he was a very interesting presence. Then my brother Tony used him in *Crimson Tide*." For his part, Mortensen found his casting in *G. I. Jane* to be painless, unlike the training which would follow. "I just met

Ridley and got the job. It was flattering to be cast without any apparent hesitation on his part in such an important role. I am very grateful to him." In order to accurately depict the Naval Special Operations training practices, Mortensen went to the Naval Base in Coronado, California where he watched the actual training and talked to as many active and retired SEALs as he could. Describing the character he finally developed, the actor said: "I am the law and all must obey or suffer the dire consequences."

"We took a very aggressive stance in the training programme," explained military technical advisor Harry Humphries. "We tried to show the harassment of the Special Forces training and the skills, including weapons handling, that are taught in that training. We encapsulated a 17-week course into two weeks, so those actors were harassed to hell." Humphries was impressed by Demi Moore, "On the first day of training I saw this young woman out there with the rest of the troops getting muddy doing push-ups and sit-ups and squat-jumps and running around obstacles. I said, 'That's a great stunt double,' so I walked up to her and said, 'You've got a lot of guts.' That night we were introduced, and the person I had thought was the stunt double was Demi!"

Moore actually considered the training a bonus to being in *G. I. Jane.* "I could have come in and asked to let the stuntwoman do the obstacle course," Moore admitted. "But I felt I would have walked away having missed an opportunity experiencing, first-hand, what these people actually go through in training; it's the whole reason for doing this film in the first place. I didn't want any special treatment just because of who I am or my position in the film. It was interesting to step into the real-life experiences of what the SEALs go through."

As well as taking part in the physical training, Demi Moore had another ritual in common with the men of *G. I. Jane.* She, too, had to shave her head in the military style. "One of the big moments after reading the script was the impact of the scene where Lt. O'Neil cuts off her hair," Moore remembered. "It's an integral part of the story and reflects her total commitment. I had five or six months before we reached the point of filming that scene and when the time came, I was ready to do it in order to get on with the real down and dirty part of the training."

After the scene was shot, the assembled group of men cheered in approval. "It was interesting," Moore continued, "I had more people want to touch me. The funniest responses came from my children who would say to friends, 'Hey, do you want to come look at my Mom's head?' as if I were a show-and-tell item. Even my husband (Bruce Willis) had a laugh."

The film was largely shot in Florida, including in Camp Blanding, a state-owned military reservation. The 30,000 acre National Guard training site was ideal for the purposes of shooting this military tale, with its pine forests, lakes and real military barracks, rifle ranges and heliports. When the filming was scheduled to start there was one big problem: the 8,000 National Guardsmen who were on manoeuvres at Camp Blanding. As a result, the production lost half its preparation time, including the work required to extend some of the buildings and create a beach. "The art department was very creative in turning an inland location into a beach," commented location manager Mary Morgan. "In reality, our beach with the dunes was an hour's drive away."

Reception: Like *Thelma & Louise* before it, *G. I. Jane* provoked a huge amount of controversy concerning the roles of women in modern American society. Reviews and articles exploited this angle in taking a position on the film. *The Chicago-Sun Times* critic Roger Ebert claimed to have seen through the ruse: 'As he did in the similarly shrewd yet feather-brained *Thelma & Louise*, the director, Ridley Scott, may even be able to convince people they're seeing a risky treatment of a controversial issue. In *G. I. Jane*, as in *Thelma & Louise*, the moments held up as feminist triumphs are when women imitate the worst of male behaviour.' *The San Francisco Chronicle* took an altogether more positive view of Scott's second feminist themed movie: 'As Scott demonstrated in *Thelma & Louise*, he has a feel for strong female characters. He brings out Moore's best quality: a don't-mess-with-me feistiness.'

6. Heroes And Villains

Gladiator (2000)

"In this life or the next, I will have my vengeance."

– Maximus, *Gladiator*.

Director: Ridley Scott, Writer: Daniel Franzoni (Story), Daniel Franzoni, John Logan & William Nicholson (Screenplay)

Cast: Russell Crowe (Maximus Decimus Meridius), Joaquin Phoenix (Commodus), Connie Nielsen (Lucilla), Oliver Reed (Proximo), Richard Harris (Marcus Aurelius), Derek Jacobi (Gracchus), Djimon Hounsou (Juba), David Schofield (Falco), John Shrapnel (Gaius), Tomas Arana (Quintus), Ralph Moeller (Hagen), Spencer Treat Clark (Lucius), David Hemmings (Cassius), Tommy Flanagan (Cicero), Sven-Ole Thorsen (Tigris), Gianina Facio (Maximus' Wife), Giorgio Cantarini (Maximus' Son)

Crew: Producers: David H Franzoni, Branko Lustig, Laurie MacDonald (Executive), Terry Needham (Associate), Walter F Parkes (Executive), Douglas Wick; Music: Hans Zimmer, Klaus Badelt (Additional Music), Lisa Gerrard (Additional Music); Cinematography: John Mathieson; Editing: Pietro Scalia; Production Design: Arthur Max; Art Direction: Keith Pain; Costume Design: Janty Yates; Visual Effects: Mill Film Ltd

Plot: AD 180. Emperor Marcus Aurelius is dying. He appoints his best general, Maximus, as 'Protector of Rome' until it can again become a Republic. However, the emperor's unstable son, Commodus, wants the throne and kills his father in order to take his place. Commodus orders the death of Maximus, as well as that of his wife and child. Escaping with his life, unlike his wife and child, Maximus becomes a gladiator, fighting his way back to Rome to get close to the emperor and gain his revenge.

Inspiration: Ridley Scott was in no hurry to follow up *G. I. Jane* with another movie. With his company Scott Free giving him the opportunity to produce films he didn't want to direct, Scott took his time and waited for the right screenplay. His producing chores included the black comedy *Clay Pigeons* (1998), the Paul Newman caper movie *Where The Money Is* (2000), and *RKO 281* (1999), a made-for-HBO TV movie about Orson Welles and the making of *Citizen Kane*. So taken by the potential of the last film was Scott that he briefly considered directing it as a feature film, before handing the reins over to Ben Ross (*The Young Poisoners Handbook*).

Scott developed *I Am Legend*, based on Richard Matheson's SF novel, as a directorial project. The book chronicles the adventures of the last human left alive after a biological war as he battles the undead vampires which his fellow humans have become. The story had been filmed twice before as *The Last Man On Earth* (1964), starring Vincent Price and as *The Omega Man* (1971), starring Charlton Heston. Warner Bros. backed the development of this new version of Matheson's tale, and Scott managed to get ageing action star Arnold Schwarzenegger attached. However, as the proposed budget started to climb over $100 million, Warners got cold feet and pulled the plug on the project. In some ways this came as a relief to Scott who felt that the script he'd inherited needed much more work before it could become a film he'd be comfortable working on. Soon after the collapse of *I Am Legend*, Ridley Scott found himself involved in the early development of another dramatic adventure movie entitled *Gladiator*.

The film began for Scott with a painting. Executive producer and co-head of DreamWorks Pictures Walter Parkes, along with producer Douglas Wick, walked into Scott's office and showed him 'Pollice Verso' (Thumbs Down) by the 19th Century artist Jean-Léon Gérôme. A Roman gladiator stands at the centre of the great Coliseum looking up at the emperor, awaiting his decision. With the power of life or death, the emperor's thumb is outstretched, and the monarch's expression unforgiving. He appears poised to signal the gladiator to kill his defeated opponent. "That image spoke to me of the Roman Empire in all its glory and wickedness," said Scott. "I knew right then and there I was hooked."

Fortunately for the director, Parkes also had a screenplay entitled *Gladiator*, written by David Franzoni, John Logan and William Nicholson. Wick explained: "About two years ago, David Franzoni came to me wanting to do a movie set in ancient Rome. We started doing the research and discovered that almost every aspect of the culture revolved around the arena. It was at the epicentre of all levels of society, and, in support of it, huge breakthroughs were made in architecture, in metalwork, in drainage... almost everything imaginable. The more we learned, the more convinced we were that the arena would be an amazing place to set a story."

Gladiator was a throwback to an older style of movie, including classics like *Spartacus, Ben Hur, The Fall Of The Roman Empire* and other Roman gladiator sword 'n' sandal epics. Ridley Scott's attraction to the film was simple and straightforward: "*Gladiator* excited me because it unfolded in a world completely different from the ones I'd previously explored. I loved the costume drama of it all and remembered that world vividly [from previous films]. I also knew that you've got to reinvent it." He was also wary of tackling a genre which was somewhat out of fashion. "There have been too many *Airplane*-style references about gladiators. All that passes through one's mind, because one likes to avoid the toga and sandal syndrome. So I think I had my eye on that at all times. However, I thought doing the Roman Empire again was a great idea. We haven't seen that for 40 years, since *Spartacus*."

There was also a political dimension, a concern with the society of the film, an element which had informed some of his best films, including *Alien* and *Blade Runner*. Scott noted: "Entertainment has frequently been used as a tool of leaders, as a means to distract an abused citizenry. The most tyrannical ruler must still beguile his people even as he brutalises them. The gladiatorial games were such a distraction. Our story suggests that, should a hero arise out of the carnage of the arena, his popularity would give him tremendous power... and were he to be a genuine champion of the people, he might threaten even the most absolute tyrant."

Cast: The film-makers behind *Gladiator* knew that the actor chosen to portray Maximus, the general-turned-gladiator whose popularity threatens the power of the emperor was key to the success of the project. "Maximus is the very soul of the movie," producer Douglas Wick claimed. "It was crucial to find an actor who you could believe possessed the ferocity of this great warrior, but in whom you could also see a man of strong principle and character. Russell Crowe's name came up pretty fast. His intensity, his dignity and his utter conviction in every role made him everyone's first choice."

Starring as Maximus, Russell Crowe takes on a decidedly different role from his Oscar-nominated turn in *The Insider*. "He went from being a paunchy, middle-aged man to a gladiator – not bad," Scott maintained, pointing out that Crowe was, "in other words, a real actor. Russell has an uncanny way of internalising a role, and he's naturally very physical, which was a perfect combination."

The downsizing Maximus suffers was at the centre of the character's arc as Crowe saw it. "He was a military man who fought for honour and the glory of Rome, but now he has to bring himself to kill on a much more base level. For a while, he lives only to stand in front of the new emperor and exact his revenge, but he is again caught up in the political turmoil of the day, and can't help but become involved. For want of a better expression, he's a good man."

The man upon whom Maximus seeks his revenge is Commodus, who becomes the emperor of Rome upon the death of Marcus Aurelius. It was important to the drama that Maximus' strength be counterbalanced by an equal measure of power on the part of his adversary, albeit another kind of power. Despite first considering British actor Jude Law, the film-makers found what they were looking for embodied in the quiet intensity of Joaquin Phoenix, brother of the late River Phoenix. Ridley Scott had previously worked with Phoenix when he executive produced the film *Clay Pigeons*, in which the actor had starred. "When we offered him the part, I think the most surprised person was Joaquin himself," the director said. "He is not the physically imposing type one might have envisioned in the role, but he conveys the complexities of this corrupt ruler in a very courageous way. He exposes the vulnerability that is juxtaposed with the ruthlessness of Commodus."

Phoenix reflected upon Commodus: "I think the best way to describe him is as a spoiled child. He's 19 years old, but wields an incredible amount of power, so he has all the emotions that go with being that age without having had the guidance he needed to handle that power. He's vulnerable and sad one moment and throwing a tantrum the next. He desperately wants the love of the people, but the irony of the story is that the gladiatorial games he decrees to get the masses to love him are ultimately what bring his nemesis to Rome."

The person closest to Commodus is his sister Lucilla, played by Connie Nielsen. "The script completely gripped me," Nielsen explained. "There are colossal elements, like the setting and the battles, and yet the story is very intimate in how it brings you into the personal relationships between people, especially in the case of Lucilla. She is caught between the ambitions of her brother and the will of Maximus, with whom she has a past."

The main cast of *Gladiator* included several respected veterans of the stage and screen, including: Richard Harris as emperor Marcus Aurelius, who understands the depths of his failings as a father too late to save his empire from tragedy; Derek Jacobi as Senator Gracchus, who sees the corruption of Commodus' reign; and the late Oliver Reed as the gladiator trainer Proximo. As Scott pointed out, "These actors are of a generation that experienced some of those earlier epics first-hand, particularly Richard." Harris said, "It was also a smashing part for me, because I love playing introspective characters. Marcus is a man in crisis, wrestling with demons. He was a scholar and a philosopher, but he spent 16 of his 20 years as emperor fighting battles and spilling blood to expand the empire. Now nearing the end, he has come to the realisation that his life was a fraud."

In his last screen role, Oliver Reed played Proximo, the man who teaches Maximus the advantages of being a gladiator who wins the hearts of the crowd. It is at Proximo's training camp that Maximus also learns important lessons about life and death from another enslaved gladiator, Juba, with whom he develops a strong bond.

Djimon Hounsou (*Amistad*), who played Juba, said of his character, "Juba knows that being a gladiator means killing or being killed. He is a very skilful fighter, which enables him to stay alive physically, but he knows a way to stay alive mentally and spiritually as well. In his mind, he is with his people; his loved ones are there, waiting for him. That ability to find freedom in your mind is something he tries to share with Maximus."

Production: From the dramatic opening battle, through to the contests in the gladiatorial arena itself, this was to be an action-packed film like no other directed by Ridley Scott. The opening battle, supposedly on the Germanic front, was shot in Surrey, England and was meticulously planned. "First of all, you come up with a battle plan. You come up with the logic, because battles can get really boring. I learned this on *The Duellists*. That film took five encounters. So I sat down quite coldly and worked out that each one would be entirely different, because waving a sword around gets very similar. There's only a few moves that you can actually make, so each battle must have an idea. The big battle plan at the beginning must have strategy. You have catapults, which are basically firing canisters of oil, which will saturate the ground with what you call Greek fire. You would then ignite that oil with flaming arrows from the archers. But then I thought, 'How would the archer do this? Each one doesn't have a cigarette lighter.' We figured there's gotta be a trench. This is where you use conjecture. So I had them dig a trench, fill it with oil, then these two powder-monkeys would run along and light them. That way, every archer would have a trench in front of them with fire, so once the general yells, 'Fire at will,' your archers can take their arrow, dip it in, and fire at will. So if you have a plan, the scene has a drama to it, rather than just people wailing at each other with swords. The gladiatorial contests, of course, are easier to work out in terms of their story. Each one has a little story."

Despite the graphic nature of each of the encounters in the film, it is the story which is central and each battle or event is used by the director to move the story on. "The story and the characters are always developed first and then gradually as I get into the process of making the movie I make changes to the script, as they are needed." It was by thinking Maximus' story through that Scott came up with a new ending. "We talked a lot about the journey of this particular character, and his history," noted Scott. "It seemed to me that a professional soldier inevitably must think about death. So his demise could be imminent at any time. So I then associate to him the fact that he's a farmer as well, and all he wants to do is go home. So then came the idea of him squatting in the mud before every encounter, and taking the mud and smelling it, because this is where he may end."

The opening and closing shots of the film, Maximus in a wheat field, seemingly returning home, were last minute additions slotted in to bring the beginning and end of the movie together. "The idea of the wheat came about when I was standing at the end of the movie in Tuscany. And I was staring at the wheat, as an afterthought I got the guy with the steady-cam to knock off the double of Russell walking through the wheat. I said 'just stroke the wheat.' So we shot that, and I knew it was exactly what I had been looking for. It starts the film off, and virtually ends the film. It's also relating to home. In his terms, standing there on that battlefield when he's feeling a bit damp, his feet are wet, and he's about to go into another battle. I think he's just thinking about home. And then if you take the scene where he describes home, what he's actually describing to Marcus Aurelius is Heaven. Because that's the perfect place."

One of the most memorable confrontations in the arena includes a fight which featured two pairs of ferocious tigers. Scott was concerned about putting his leading man in danger. "The danger with a big tabby like that, who is 600 pounds and nine feet long, is that for the most part you want to go over and hug him. Once one of those tigers is on you, it can be over in a few seconds. One of the tigers forgot who was boss, and bit his master, who had steel cuffs on. He bit him – he closed his jaws lightly on him, but it left a hole in the metal about the size of a quarter."

Fearing that the actor might injure himself, thus causing problems for the production, the producers sent Crowe a memo forbidding him from playing football during the shooting period. "That was funny," remembered Crowe. "They'd let me run in front of chariots, wrestle tigers and do battle with 5000 men in the snow and mud. The memo I sent back was, 'I can wrestle four tigers, but I can't play soccer? Get over it. Love, Russell.'"

Gladiator was not a problem-free production. From reported bad behaviour of the lead actor through to storms in Malta, Scott had his work cut out for him to keep this production on the road. Crowe reportedly got into 'brawls' with villagers, wrecked his rented villa in Morocco (causing the caretaker to complain to Scott: "He must leave! He is violating every tenet of the Koran!"), questioned many aspects of the script and even stormed off the set when he didn't get his own way. One DreamWorks executive claimed: "Russell was not well behaved. He tried to rewrite the entire script on the spot. You know the big line in the trailer: 'In this life or the next, I will have my vengeance!' At first, he absolutely refused to say it. He did a

82

lot of posturing and put the fear of God into some people. Thankfully, Ridley never yelled. He was the voice of reason, dealing with many unreasonable factors, not the least of which was his lead." Scott had obviously learned much about dealing with egomaniac actors and out-of-control films since *Blade Runner*.

Production designer Arthur Max had his own problems, nothing to do with the actors. "We couldn't control the weather," he said of location shooting on Malta, "and we couldn't control the politics. We came in the midst of an election during which everyone [in power] we'd been dealing with was voted out of office, and our permits went with them. Parts of the set were destroyed by storms and a lot of the materials we were having shipped in couldn't reach us because the ships couldn't enter the port."

As well as using computer-generated imagery to recreate ancient Rome, the Coliseum and to enhance the battle and action scenes, Ridley Scott found himself using it for a much more simple task: to bring back actor Oliver Reed who died during shooting. Reed was a wild man of British cinema, an actor who'd never lived up to his promise and had developed a tabloid reputation for spending more time drinking than working. Ironically, Reed died in a pub in Malta a week before completing his shooting on *Gladiator*, in which he played Maximus' trainer Proximo. "When it came to insuring actors," said Producer Douglas Wick, "the only person over whom there was a little question was Oliver Reed, and unfortunately that turned out to be prescient."

Nikki Penny, visual effects supervisor at Mill Film Ltd, the effects house owned by Ridley Scott which created all the effects for *Gladiator*, found himself having to tackle this most unusual task. "We just took Ollie from one scene and placed him into another. The sequence we fabricated is when Proximo walks towards Maximus' slave-school cell to free him. We used an earlier take of Ollie in another scene, rotoscoped him out and positioned him into the new plate. We lit it, gave him a haircut and a digital shave, because he had a full beard in the take we used. We turned the beard into a goatee and replaced the skin by blending an extras face into his jawline."

Ridley Scott had hoped to include Oliver Reed in the ending of the film, a scene which wasn't to be due to the actor's death. "We always thought Ollie was a man for all seasons – he was a magnificent survivor. At the end of it all, despite everything he did, you kind of liked him. The idea was to see Oliver, at the end of it all, go off into the wilderness, back to Morocco, and take one look back at Rome, and shrug and move on. One wanted to feel at that moment that Oliver was, to a certain extent, a changed man. But we couldn't do that."

Reception: Glowing reviews and a stunning success at the box office for *Gladiator* proved that Ridley Scott was back on form. After a series of less interesting, flop movies, he'd finally directed a film which ranks up there with his best work, with *Alien, Blade Runner* and *Legend*. Between its release in May and the end of October 2000, *Gladiator* drew in over $190 million at the American box office, totalling over $434 million world-wide.

'What's enjoyable about *Gladiator*, is how it plays mischievously with the idea that moviegoers are just modernised, bloodthirsty Roman rabble,' said *The Washington Post*, commenting on the way the audience found themselves caught up in Scott's period film. According to *The San Francisco Chronicle* 'This Ridley Scott film, his best in years, re-envisions ancient Rome for 2000 and makes it safe to go back in the Coliseum. Scott never ceases giving us interesting things to look at, including Rome: seen for the first time by the gladiators, it looks as glittering and assaultive. This may be the first Roman epic ever where the audience is made to understand the sensory impact of just entering the arena.' In *Gladiator, The LA Times* recognised another of Ridley Scott's fully realised worlds: 'If Crowe is well suited to be this film's star, the same can be said for Ridley Scott as its director. From *The Duellists*, his 1977 debut, through classics like *Alien* and *Blade Runner*, Scott has demonstrated a wonderful gift for ambience, for making out-of-the-ordinary worlds come alive on screen."

Facts And Figures:

• The rose petals which litter the gladiatorial arena are in fact petals from Remembrance Day poppies. The order by the producers for the poppy petals set back production for Remembrance Day by three months.

• It took 100 British technicians, 200 Maltese tradesmen and 19 weeks to construct the one-third circumference recreation of Rome's ancient Coliseum in Malta. Up to 3000 extras were used to fill the Coliseum's 52-foot-high set. Computer graphic effects were then used to add the remainder of the Coliseum which had not been built on location and create a further 33,000 bloodthirsty spectators. The computer-generated 3D model of the Coliseum used the exact measurements of the original.

• Among the cut scenes scripted but never filmed for *Gladiator* were the training scene between Maximus and the rhino (the CG work and prosthetics would have added $3 million to the budget) and a battle with blind albino Africans who blend into the arena walls and whom Maximus tricks into fighting each other.

- Like modern-day athletes, ancient Roman gladiators did product endorsements. "Gladiators endorsed products," producer Douglas Wick claimed. "But if you cut to Russell Crowe endorsing a chariot or olive oil, that would become parody when in fact it's true." However, while the producers considered including this in the script, they finally discarded the idea as unbelievable.

- Connie Nielsen found a 2000-year-old signet ring in an antique store, which she wears in the movie.

- Russell Crowe began shooting for *Gladiator* a few months after *The Insider* wrapped. He had gained upwards of 40 pounds for his Oscar-nominated role in *The Insider* and yet lost it all before *Gladiator* began. He claims he did nothing special other than normal work on his sheep farm in Australia.

Hannibal (2001)

"The Silence Will Be Broken."

– Teaser Tagline, *Hannibal*.

Director: Ridley Scott, Writers: Thomas Harris (Novel), Steve Zaillian (Screenwriter)

Cast: Anthony Hopkins (Dr. Hannibal Lecter), Julianne Moore (Clarice Starling), Gary Oldman (Mason Verger), Ray Liotta (FBI Agent Paul Krendler), Giancarlo Giannini (Rinaldo Pazzi), Diane Baker (Senator Ruth Martin), Boyd Kestner (Mendez), Zeljko Ivanek (Cordell), Ivano Marescotti (Carlos Deogracias), Franke Faison (Barney), Spike Jonze (Donnie Barber), Sam Wells (TV Anchorman)

Crew: Producers: Dino De Laurentiis, Martha De Laurentiis, Ridley Scott, Branko Lustig (Executive); Director of Photography: John Mathieson; Editor: Pietro Scalia; Music: Hans Zimmer; Production Designer: Norris Spencer; Art Direction: David Crank; Costume Designer: Janty Yates

Plot: Mason Verger, disfigured tycoon and sole survivor of an attack by Dr. Hannibal 'The Cannibal' Lecter, places a bounty on the infamous psychiatrist's head, hoping to exact a terrible revenge upon him. Special Agent Clarice Starling, suspended from the FBI and under close scrutiny from men wishing to discredit her, is hired by Verger and unwittingly becomes a pawn in his deadly trap.

Inspiration: By June 1999, just as *Gladiator* was enjoying its biggest success in cinemas around the world, it appeared that Ridley Scott had found a new film to direct: the sequel to the 1991 Oscar-winning serial-killer thriller, *The Silence Of The Lambs*. It would be the first time that Scott would tackle a sequel to another film-makers work. "Partly it was the designer in me wanting to explore new worlds," said Scott of his interest in *Hannibal*, "but I'm only attracted by material that rings my bell. *Hannibal* is a great story."

Producer Dino De Laurentiis, who had long ago approached Scott to direct his film version of Frank Herbert's *Dune* had paid $10 million to acquire the film rights to Thomas Harris' long-anticipated novel, the follow-up to his previous thrillers *Red Dragon* (filmed as *Manhunter*) and *The Silence Of The Lambs*.

Scott, however, was aware that he was at least the second choice for the job, as Jonathan Demme (who directed *The Silence Of The Lambs*) dropped out, claiming he couldn't compete with himself. "I read it and my first question was 'What about Jonathan [Demme]," said Scott of his introduction to *Hannibal*. "The answer was that Jonathan had a difference with the story and there was a general feeling that the character was a bit too violent. The reason that I took it was all to do with the book, and violence is really how you serve it up" According to Industry trade papers, Demme felt Harris' sequel novel was too violent and wanted changes the author would not permit.

The new novel, simply entitled *Hannibal* and featuring a bizarre conclusion which links Clarice Starling and Hannibal Lecter in a romantic way, was a best-seller. When Scott signed on to make the film, there was no agreement in place to bring back the stars of the previous film: Anthony Hopkins (who played Hannibal) or Jodie Foster (who played FBI agent Clarice Starling).

There was even speculation that De Laurentiis didn't want Foster in the new film, but he may have been preparing the way for Foster's expected refusal to play the role. For her part, Foster expressed distaste with the conclusion of the new book, but maintained that she'd wait for a screenplay before deciding. Additionally, no screenwriter had been hired, and Universal Pictures, which also had ties to the film rights, had not confirmed that it would release the movie sequel. Scott clearly faced an uphill struggle to bring this project back together.

Anthony Hopkins, who won his Oscar for his role as the psycho psychiatrist, bit first and approved the script by Steven Zaillian (an Oscar winner himself for his *Schindler's List* screenplay). Zaillian was brought onboard to rework a previous attempt to adapt the novel by acclaimed writer-director David Mamet. Zaillian's script had a radically different ending from Thomas Harris' novel. Hopkins loved the script and a deal was made.

Jodie Foster continued to prevaricate, despite Hopkins' confirmed involvement. She even admitted in *W* magazine: "I stand to make more money doing that sequel that I ever have in my life, but who cares, if it betrays Clarice – who is a person, in some strange way, to me." She continued to object to the end of the novel which saw Clarice and Lecter run away together and invite a friend over for dinner... "The movie worked because people believed in her heroism," Foster told *W*. "I won't play her with negative attributes she'd never have."

By November 1999, Foster finally decided to bail out on *Hannibal*, claiming she was opting out of the project to direct a movie of her own (entitled *Flora Plum* and starring Claire Danes). The role of Clarice Starling had still to be filled.

Ridley Scott, however, managed to pull a casting surprise out of the hat by persuading acclaimed actress Julianne Moore to take on the role of Starling. Moore, who'd drawn rave critical notices for her roles in *The End Of The Affair* and *Magnolia*, reportedly beat out Gillian Anderson, Helen Hunt, Cate Blanchett, Angelina Jolie, Hilary Swank and Calista Flockhart to the role.

Production: Hopkins and Moore were joined by Gary Oldman and Ray Liotta when shooting began in Italy on 8 April 2000. Oldman (*Lost In Space*) won the role of Mason Verger, disfigured and vengeful as a result of a previous, near-lethal encounter with Dr Hannibal Lecter, while Liotta (*Goodfellas*), took on the part of a senior FBI agent.

The five-week location shoot started in Florence, Italy, before moving to Washington, USA. At a press conference on the first day of shooting, Scott spoke about changing the end of the film from that of the novel. "The ending was always a big question," he said. "I just couldn't accept it." Scott added, however, that he had *Hannibal* author Thomas Harris' approval for his modified ending, which he claimed retains the spirit of the book. "I think it's correct for the film but I'm not going to reveal what it is. Steve [Zaillian] had a difficult task adapting the book. It's not easy condensing 600 pages into a script and still retaining the spirit."

Julianne Moore admitted she was nervous about following in Jodie Foster's footsteps, but added that, "the new Clarice would be very different. Of course people are going to compare my interpretation with that of Jodie Foster's, which was wonderful, but the film is going to be very different...

the biggest change is that it's ten years on. In *Silence Of The Lambs* Clarice was a student – in *Hannibal* she has a lot more authority. She's moved on."

Julianne Moore spent several weeks in FBI basic training, learning how to track down criminals, run like a FBI agent, as well as how to use handcuffs and handle a gun. According to insiders at the 650-acre Quantico-based camp, the actress "brightened up the training" for the hundreds of other would-be FBI agents she joined. Spokesman for the FBI base Kirk Crawford recalled: "To train Julianne we had to get special permission from our headquarters. It was quite an unusual request... The thing is we train all the FBI agents out here and so we really hate it when we see people playing FBI agents in the movies and getting it all wrong. It is misinformation so we are happy to have given her basic training. She learnt how to handcuff and how an agent would act or think in a given situation."

Wrapping the production, Ridley Scott said of his final cut of *Hannibal*, "I'm very pleased. It's fantastic, and I'm very happy with the whole group of actors, they were really great. Julianne was just fantastic and Tony is a sweetheart. I learnt more with Tony during the summer than in the last few of my movies..."

While audiences have not yet had a chance to react to the unusual developments between Starling and Lecter in the film, Scott was convinced that his version of the novel would work. "I saw the book as a highly-entertaining continuation of the relationship between Hannibal and Clarice, to the point where he virtually declares to her his support and undying faith. I found that interesting."

Facts And Figures:

• *Hannibal*, with a budget of $80 million started shooting in Florence on 8 May for five weeks, followed by a brief location shoot in Sardinia before returning to the United States to film in Washington, Richmond and North Carolina. In a neat touch that Lecter himself would be proud of, the film was due to be released in the States on Valentine's Day 2001.

7. New Worlds

What next for Ridley Scott? None of his previous movies had brought Scott the power to choose the best of the available scripts for his next project. Now, after *Gladiator* and *Hannibal* he could. "I do think that for the first 10 years [as a movie director] I spent too much time waiting or developing, or being too critical about what I would take on next," admitted Scott towards the end of 2000, as he faced selecting his next project. "At the end of the day, it's a movie, not a cure for cancer. We're entertainers and I learned to lighten up."

Having done one sequel in *Hannibal,* Scott found himself contemplating another: *Terminator 3*. The attraction for Scott was that this film would feature a female Terminator as a protagonist: the ultimate Ridley Scott 'strong woman'. "I've decided that sometimes you can dwell too long, too often on what will be the 'next subject' and I now feel it's best just to get on with it. Just do it, that's my motto."

Rather than wait, the 62-year-old Scott, decided to direct *Black Hawk Down*, a tale based on the shooting down of an American helicopter during the American involvement in Somalia in 1993. While that high concept pitch might sound like the Matt Damon-starring Gulf War film *Courage Under Fire* or even *Rules Of Engagement*, it is certain that Scott's movie would have been a unique look at the American military in dramatic action. The source for that film was Mark Bowden's 1999 'non-fiction novel' called *Black Hawk Down: A Story Of Modern War*. The book covered the battle of Mogadishu, the longest sustained ground battle to involve American forces since the Vietnam War. Mark Bowden worked on a script for the movie which was then redrafted by Ken Nolan. Jerry Bruckheimer was in the producer's chair (he had previously worked with Scott's brother, Tony Scott) and Scott expected to start production in February 2001. Already cast in the movie were Josh Hartnett (*Pearl Harbour*), Tom Sizemore (*Red Planet*) and Australian actor Eric Bana. Release was pencilled in for November 2001.

After that, Scott hoped to tackle a film version of Ben Elton's novel and stage play *Popcorn*, where movie violence spills into real life when a couple kidnap a film director. There was also the possibility of Scott returning to Hannibal Lecter once again. Even before the second film had been released, there was talk of Scott helming an adaptation of Thomas Harris' *Red Dragon*, previously filmed by Michael Mann as *Manhunter* which featured Brian Cox in the Lecter role. Both Scott and star Anthony Hopkins confirmed they would at least look at the script for a third outing. Writer Ted Tally was hard at work on the script by the end of 2000.

Scott needs to concentrate on the movie-making, rather than on his business interests. Arguably, his concentration on business (like Shepperton, Mill Film Ltd and RSA) may have led to films like *White Squall* being less than they could have been. It's an analysis which David Puttnam would agree with: "I always thought that if Ridley had concentrated solely on making movies he would have a clutch of Oscars under his belt, because he certainly has the talent. He has just allowed himself, all too often, to get distracted. I just wish he devoted more time to his film-making because along the way there have been films that didn't do his talent justice. In his oeuvre, there are half a dozen really great movies. All I'm saying is, that there should have been a dozen, because he had it in him."

For Ridley Scott, issuing advice to new film-makers, his purpose as a movie director and the way to achieve it was clear: "For me, the challenge is always to create a world, to establish characters and tell a story. My message to them is just have a go. Just do it."

8. Resource Materials

Films As Director

Hannibal (2001)

Gladiator (2000)

G. I. Jane (1997)

White Squall (1996)

1492: Conquest Of Paradise (1992)

Thelma & Louise (1991)

Black Rain (1989)

Someone To Watch Over Me (1987)

Legend (1985)

Blade Runner (1982)

Alien (1979)

The Duellists (1977)

Other Films As Producer

Where The Money Is (2000)

Clay Pigeons (1998)

Monkey Trouble (1994)

The Browning Version (1994)

Television

RKO 281 (1999) TV Movie, Producer

The Hunger (1997) TV Series, Producer

Adam Adamant Lives! (1966) TV Series, Director

Out Of The Unknown (1965) TV Series, Production Designer

R3 (1964) TV Series, Production Designer

Softly, Softly (1962) TV Series, Director

Video/DVD

UK (VHS video & DVD Region 2 Releases)

The Duellists (1977)

Alien (1979)

Alien (1979) Box Set, also includes *Aliens, Alien3 & Alien Resurrection*

Blade Runner (1982), VHS

Blade Runner (Director's Cut Special Edition, 1992), VHS

Blade Runner (Director's Cut Special Edition, 1992), DVD

Legend (1985), VHS

Someone To Watch Over Me (1987), DVD

Black Rain (1989), VHS

Black Rain (1989), DVD

Thelma & Louise (1991), DVD And Booklet

Thelma & Louise (1991), VHS

1492: Conquest Of Paradise (1992), VHS

White Squall (1996), VHS

G. I. Jane (1996), DVD

Gladiator (2000), Gift Box VHS Video, CD And Book

Gladiator (2000), VHS

Gladiator (2000), DVD (Two Disc Set)

US: Region 1 DVD Releases

Alien (1979)

The *Alien* Legacy (*Alien* films box set, 1979-1997)

Blade Runner - Limited Edition Collector's Set (1982)

Blade Runner - The Director's Cut (1982)

Legend (Collector's Edition) (1986)

Someone To Watch Over Me (1987)

Black Rain (1989)

Thelma & Louise (1991)

White Squall (1996)

G. I. Jane (1997)

Gladiator (2000)

Books

Alien: The Complete Illustrated Screenplay by Dan O'Bannon, Ridley Scott (Introduction), Orion Hardcover (Published 2000).

Gladiator: The Making Of The Ridley Scott Epic by Ridley Scott, Walter Parkes, Boxtree (Published 2000)

Ridley Scott by Paul M Sammon, Orion Paperback (Published 2000)

H R Giger's Film Design by H R Giger (Illustrator), Ridley Scott (Introduction), Titan Books Paperback (Published 1996)

Future Noir: The Making Of Blade Runner by Paul M Sammon, Harper-Prism. paperback (Published 1996)

Articles

Liane Bonin, No Roman Holiday, *Entertainment Weekly*, May 5, 2000

Richard Corliss, The Empire Strikes Back, *Time*, May 8, 2000 Vol. 155 No. 19

James Inverne, The Talented Mr. Ridley, *Time*, June 26, 2000 Vol. 155 No. 25

Mark Morris, Done Roman, *The Observer*, May 7, 2000

Dan Peary, Directing Alien And Blade Runner: An Interview With Ridley Scott, *Omni Screenflights/Screen Fantasies*, Doubleday, 1984

Press Notes for Alien, Blade Runner, Legend, Someone To Watch Over Me, Black Rain, Thelma & Louise, 1492: Conquest Of Paradise, White Squall, G. I. Jane, Gladiator

TV Interviews

Russell Crowe, *Entertainment Tonight*, Paramount Pictures, May 5, 2000

Ridley Scott Interview, *Entertainment Tonight*, Paramount Pictures, May 12, 2000

Websites

The Ridley Scott Fan Information Page: http://www.angelfire.com/movies/ridleyscott/

Legend Frequently Asked Questions: http://www.figmentfly.com/legend/index.shtml

Ridley Scott @ Internet Movie Database: http://us.imdb.com/M/person-exact?+Scott,+Ridley

Blade Runner: :http://www.bit.net.au/~muzzle/bladerunner/

The Universe Of Blade Runner: http://www.multimania.com/iambladerunner/index2.html?

2019: Off-World (*Blade Runner* Page): http://scribble.com/uwi/br/off-world.html

Lycos Directory: Website List For Alien: http://dir.lycos.com/Arts/Movies/Series/Alien/

Ridley Scott Interview, Dayna D'Itria, *www.iCast.com*

E! Online coverage of Hannibal

The Essential Library

Why not try other titles in the Pocket Essentials library? Each is £2.99 unless otherwise stated. Look out for new titles every month.

New: **Ridley Scott** by Brian J Robb (£3.99)
Billy Wilder by Glenn Hopp (£3.99)

Film: **Woody Allen** by Martin Fitzgerald
Jane Campion by Ellen Cheshire
Jackie Chan by Michelle Le Blanc & Colin Odell
Joel & Ethan Coen by John Ashbrook & Ellen Cheshire
David Cronenberg by John Costello (£3.99)
Film Noir by Paul Duncan
Terry Gilliam by John Ashbrook
Heroic Bloodshed edited by Martin Fitzgerald
Alfred Hitchcock by Paul Duncan
Krzysztof Kieslowski by Monika Maurer
Stanley Kubrick by Paul Duncan
David Lynch by Michelle Le Blanc & Colin Odell
Steve McQueen by Richard Luck
Marilyn Monroe by Paul Donnelley (£3.99)
The Oscars® by John Atkinson (£3.99)
Brian De Palma by John Ashbrook
Sam Peckinpah by Richard Luck
Slasher Movies by Mark Whitehead (£3.99)
Vampire Films by Michelle Le Blanc & Colin Odell
Orson Welles by Martin Fitzgerald

TV: **Doctor Who** by Mark Campbell (£3.99)

Books: **Cyberpunk** by Andrew M Butler (£3.99)
Philip K Dick by Andrew M Butler (£3.99)
Noir Fiction by Paul Duncan

Culture:**Conspiracy Theories** by Robin Ramsay (£3.99)

Available at all good bookstores, or send a cheque to: **Pocket Essentials (Dept RS), 18 Coleswood Rd, Harpenden, Herts, AL5 1EQ, UK**. Please make cheques payable to 'Oldcastle Books.' Add 50p postage & packing for each book in the UK and £1 elsewhere.

US customers can send $5.95 plus $1.95 postage & packing for each book to: **Trafalgar Square Publishing, PO Box 257, Howe Hill Road, North Pomfret, Vermont 05053, USA**. tel: 802-457-1911, fax: 802-457-1913, e-mail: tsquare@sover.net

Customers worldwide can order online at **www.pocketessentials.com**, **www.amazon.com** and at all good online bookstores.